SELF-HYPNOSIS
STEP BY STEP

SELF-HYPNOSIS STEP BY STEP

The 30 Essential Techniques

Dr J. P. Guyonnaud
with Giovanni Sciuto

Translated by Elfreda Powell

SOUVENIR PRESS

CONTENTS

Five men are sitting in a waiting-room: they have all been given appointments for the same time. Yet, as the minutes slip by, no one comes to attend to them.

Only one of them shows no sign of irritation in his demeanour. And, when his turn to be called finally arrives, the head of personnel ends his routine interview by asking:

'So, what's your secret? I was watching you and the other candidates with a hidden camera. In fact it was part of the screening process. I must admit, I was really impressed by the way you remained so calm. Tell me, how do you manage to control your temper when your patience is tested to its limits like that?'

'It's quite simple,' the candidate replies. 'I use self-hypnosis.'

'Well, it certainly works in your case. In principle, the job's yours. We'd like you to join the company.'

This example will give you an idea of the many important possible applications of self-hypnosis.

However, if this technique can be such a powerful tool in so many different situations, it is due to all the pioneering work that went on before it came into being.

Magnetism and hypnosis, from which it developed, prepared the ground for self-hypnosis to fight its corner in the medical field. So, as a starting point, it would seem useful to go back to the beginning and describe all that happened before it evolved, then trace its history up to the present day.

From 'Animal Magnetism' and Hypnosis to Self-hypnosis

The `Long March'

If we look at the techniques still used today in primitive societies, especially in Africa, the South Sea Islands and South America, it is not difficult to come to the conclusion that humans have been using magnetism and hypnosis since prehistoric times. Witch doctors, shamans and the like have traditionally relied on touching and the power of words and incantations to help cure sickness and injury, alleviate the pain of childbirth, engender courage in their hunters and warriors, or persuade someone that an evil spell has been lifted.

The oldest proof of the use of such a resource exclusively for healing can be found in the famous Ebers papyrus in the British Museum. This reveals that, in the time of the Pharaohs, a method involving the laying on of hands and verbal suggestion was among those used to alleviate or cure pain.

A lasting association

The Bible, as well as Ancient Greek and Roman histories, often alludes to these cures – miraculous or otherwise – which worked through a combination of touching and verbal incantation, intended to give the sick person a feeling of certainty that he or she would be cured.

Medieval chroniclers frequently refer to similar cases. In the laying on of hands we can see an ancient form of the therapy developed under the name of 'animal magnetism' or mesmerism, while verbal suggestion is the main force behind hypnosis.

In this way, therefore, before magnetism (as I shall refer to it from now on) or hypnosis were even spoken of, these two branches of complementary or alternative medicine remained inseparable – right up until the beginning of the nineteenth century.

Mesmer's rediscovery

Franz-Anton Mesmer (1734–1815) was the son of a forester from South-West Germany, and grew up in the countryside beside the Bodensee. He was fascinated by natural phenomena, and this fascination would remain with him throughout his life. His time at university did nothing to blunt the impact his country childhood and adolescence had had upon him, spent, as it was, in contact with 'the secret forces animating the universe'. In fact it had quite the reverse effect.

Once settled in the Austrian capital, armed with the necessary qualifications, Mesmer could have looked forward to a career teaching philosophy or practising law. He did neither. At an age when others had finished their studies, he returned to his. And this time he chose a subject that fulfilled his childhood aspirations. In 1766, at the age of 32, he acquired his third doctorate . . . this time in medicine.

He was also fortunate enough to marry a rich wife and so was able to devote his time to research. This was how he rediscovered a therapy once practised by Paracelsus in the sixteenth century: it focused the healing properties of the magnet. The conclusion he reached was that man, too, possessed magnetic energy, which could be harnessed and used to cure the sick.

His first guinea pigs were recruited from among the Viennese aristocracy, who were very much in the public eye, and from reputable scholars of the period. And he found that his experiments produced spectacular cures.

A magnet

In February 1778, by which time he was 44, Mesmer set out to conquer Paris. He knew what he was doing: scientific circles in the French capital were very open-minded, Parisians seemed to have a taste for medical innovations, and Louis XVI would surely show nothing but sympathy for an inventor who had come straight from the native city of his wife, Marie-Antoinette . . .

In part his calculations proved correct. Even if the majority of official scholars shrugged their shoulders when they heard Mesmer's explanations, or saw his practical experiments, the gentlemen and ladies of the Court were eager to try his 'miraculous cures' which everyone was talking about, while the king himself decided to grant him an allowance of twenty thousand pounds, and a sum of ten thousand pounds to train practitioners.

Very quickly Mesmer became a magnet himself for Parisian society. The middle classes followed the aristocracy's example: to be cured by the magnetism that Mesmer transmitted through his eyes, his voice and his gestures was now highly fashionable, and gossip had it that Queen Marie-Antoinette herself consulted this doctor – in a manner somewhat different from others . . .

Within a few years, Mesmer could boast not only of the total satisfaction of patients who put their entire trust in him, but also of curing a number of sceptics who had come to catch him out. Among these were several eminent scientists.

It was time, he decided, to demand official recognition for his achievements as well as more funds than he had received in the past. But Louis XVI had doubts about giving more than he already had. Affronted, Mesmer left for Flanders, leaving people in no doubt that he would return only when his methods would be given unconditional support.

Official enquiry

During Mesmer's absence, one of his old students, a Doctor Deslon, attempted to make a name for himself, but his efforts were thwarted: in 1784 two commissions were set up to provide the king with information on the merits of magnetism. However, they examined, not Mesmer's own work, but that of Dr Deslon and another professed mesmerist.

The celebrated Benjamin Franklin, Antoine Lavoisier and other illustrious scientists made up the two royal commissions; in all there were fourteen members. Physicians, chemists or doctors, they were all of the highest reputation. The experiments were carried out, and the scientific and medical luminaries established their findings, among which were the following:

'They all submitted to the man who was magnetising: however deep the apparent sleep they were in, his voice, look or gesture brought them out of it.'[1]

Accompanying that statement was the following declaration: 'Imagination can produce convulsions without magnetism, but magnetism without imagination produces nothing.'[2]

But the reports were also damning, and this was to put a brake on research into magnetism for almost two centuries:

'There is nothing to prove the existence of a magnetic fluid . . . Touching and the repeated activity of the imagination, in order to produce sudden urges, can be harmful . . .

[1] A characteristic of self-hypnosis.
[2] Auto-suggestion, an earlier development, related to hypnotism, is a concomitant of this.

Making a spectacle of these urges is dangerous, and leads to imitation, and, as a consequence, any public display of treatment in which magnetic processes are used can only have disastrous effects in the long term.'

Only Antoine-Laurent de Jussieu, the famous French botanist, refused to have anything to do with this attempted 'assassination' of magnetism. Rather than sign the accusation, which expressed the other panel members' unanimous opinion, he compiled a report of his own, drawing attention, on the one hand, to the efficacy of the magnetic treatments and to the fact that a cure was guaranteed, and, on the other, to the need to continue research into 'touching' or 'contact' within a medical framework.

Reputation in ruins

As for Mesmer, little did it matter that the royal commissions had called his competitors into question and not his own practice: his popularity dwindled. Magnetism had become associated with his name. Although the charlatans in his discipline had been weeded out by these commissions, they had, at the same time, put an end to his career on French soil. Being unable to pursue his regular consultations, he made only a few more brief visits to Paris; instead he took himself off to England and Prussia.

The final paradox

France was turned upside down by the Revolution, then by a series of wars. However, in spite of all the many problems besetting the country, some people never forgot Mesmer's teaching. These were enlightened people, the Marquis de Puységur, for example, and they continued their experiments with magnetism.

Then, peace was restored. Some old pupils of Mesmer, and high-ranking people who had not forgotten that they had been cured by him, interceded on his behalf. Napoleon

Bonaparte granted him a pension. Mesmer did not use it, however, to return to Paris to live. Rather than exposing himself to the possibility of further disappointment, he retired to his native country, to live beside the Bodensee. It was there, three years before his death, that he received the most flattering of propositions: the King of Prussia invited him to take up a professorship at the Faculty of Medicine in Berlin.

Although coming late in life, such concrete recognition of interest in his methods delighted Mesmer. But he was by then morally exhausted. In Vienna, then Paris, he had known only ephemeral success. Could he, at the age of sixty-eight, try yet again? He decided against it, preferring one of his associates to carry on the official teaching of his science. The final paradox of his life was that he ended his days curing, not the aristocracy or famous *savants* or even the wealthy middle class, but paupers whom he cared for with great devotion.

The seed germinates

Mesmer had not sown his seed in vain. There were gaps in his theories, it is true. But even then, in the nineteenth century, those very people who had good reason to fight a medical technique diametrically opposed to theirs, had to acknowledge in their inner hearts the results obtained from magnetism treatment. For this very reason, Mesmer's teachings were remembered by those whose concern was curing their fellow men. So it was that, parallel to the opening of a hospital in Berlin using Mesmer's methods to treat several hundred sick people every month, magnetism advanced in France, England and even in the Indies, opening the way to a treatment which in a very short time would develop into the healing technique we now know as hypnotism . . .

A 'divorce'?

Towards the end of the eighteenth century, research undertaken by the Marquis de Puységur identified a curious phenomenon, which was to be known as 'induced somnabulism', and which ultimately would be catalogued as one of the phenomena produced by hypnosis. After being magnetised by the marquis, one of his servants, a man called Victor, fell into a special kind of sleep, which enabled him suddenly to express himself in a very skilful manner and even go so far as to diagnose his own illness very precisely ... Others were to follow.

Several decades later, around 1810, a Portuguese magnetiser who had been born in the East Indies, a certain Abbé de Faria, became known in Paris. While his predecessors had adhered closely to the technique used by Mesmer, he simplified the process. All he did to 'condition' the subject was to place his hands for a few moments on the patient's head and shoulders. As soon as the person was sufficiently relaxed, he ordered him, in an imperious voice, to go to sleep. This 'lucid sleep' occurred often enough for Abbé de Faria to include it in his treatise, considered in the twentieth century to be the very first systematic listing of the characteristic principles of hypnosis.

In an attempt to confirm the foundations of Mesmer's teachings, another adept of magnetism, the Swiss Charles-Léonard Lafontaine (1803–92), went on a series of European tours. In an historic moment, during a public demonstration of his treatment in Manchester, he attracted the attention of the surgeon James Braid, who was to be inspired by Mesmer's method and elaborate it into a revolutionary medical technique, which he would call *hypnotism*.

Braid's researches were published in 1843. From that moment on, magnetism and hypnosis went their separate ways. But they were not truly 'divorced' because, in practice, practitioners of magnetism continued to depend on what is really a hypnotic approach, while hypnotists have always remained faithful to magnetism, especially in relation to 'magnetic passes', which are incorporated into a number of their current procedures.

However, the distinction in force in the middle of the nineteenth century between magnetism and hypnosis ended in profound upheaval; using magnetic 'fluid' for healing became the almost exclusive province of healers, while hypnosis was able to develop through the interest shown in it in medical circles.

First successes

In 1859, in a report to the Society of Surgeons in Paris, Professor Azam of Bordeaux proposed that hypnosis should replace chloroform, and that was how this new technique began its career – as a method of anaesthesia.

Still in the nineteenth century, researches into hypnosis by Dr Durand de Gros led to the birth of psychosomatic medicine: the reactions of hypnotised patients highlighted the existence of a close link between the human mind and body.

In the same period, collaboration between two doctors from Nancy in western France, a general practitioner called Liebault and a Professor Bernheim, resulted in the very first cures using modern hypnosis as a therapy.

While research by the Nancy school sensitised medical opinion on an international level, Paris, or more precisely, the Hôpital de la Salpetrière, became the theatre (and theatre is the right word here) for spectacular experiments carried out by Professor Charcot. Among those who were present at his public demonstrations of the effects that hypnosis could produce on the sick was a young Viennese doctor, by the name of Sigmund Freud . . .

And while on the subject of the future founder of psychoanalysis, it should be noted that one of his compatriots, an eminent Austrian neuropsychiatrist, Dr Breuer, who was considered along with the Frenchman, Pierre Janet, as a pioneer in the field of 'exploration of the mind', also experimented with hypnosis in the second half of the nineteenth century and demonstrated that if an illness developed from a trauma of the mind, patients could, under hypnosis, recall the original shock responsible for their illness, thus offering the doctor treating them a means of directing his healing towards the deep-seated cause of the symptoms. In other words, Dr Breuer's work showed that hypnosis could be of immense service to medicine, not only as a means of anaesthesia or healing, but it could be used with equal success in cases of psychosomatic illness, through its virtue of being able to deliver a correct diagnosis.

From agitation to calm

Magnetism practised by Mesmer provoked immediate, quite unpleasant reactions. After having simply breathed, spat and coughed, quite a number of patients ended up giving the impression that they were 'possessed: their eyes popped out, they ground their teeth, slavered, shouted out, sometimes laughing and crying, in the grip of violent convulsions'. The effect was so bad that Mesmer decided it was best to pad the walls and floor of one of his Paris consulting rooms. Patients who were the most affected by 'magnetic fits' were taken there, so that they would not hurt themselves.

To begin with, a cure was only obtained at the cost of enduring periods of 'extreme agitation'. Patients were willing to do this, however: for them, it was less painful than submitting to bloodlettings, cold baths and other medical 'tortures' typical of the period, but this particular aspect of the effects of magnetism must have provided the two royal commissions of 1784 with one of their main arguments against continuing the technique.

Later modifications to Mesmer's technique would completely eliminate inconveniences of this nature. What is more, before falling into a healthy sleep, patients experienced an agreeable sensation of heat at the point where the magnetisation was being applied, and sometimes this heat spread throughout their whole body.

By the end of the nineteenth century, magnetic techniques excluded even any sign of sleepiness, while hypnotic techniques specialised in inducing sleep, relaxation, calm . . .

Ongoing success

The beginning of the twentieth century saw an increase in the popularity of medical hypnotism.

In France, Dr Pierre Janet, a former pupil of Charcot, opened the way to more and more extensive use of hypnosis in the treatment of various illnesses. Despite the reserve shown in official medical circles, numerous practitioners became adept in hypnotherapy. Then, in the 1970s, sophrology, a method which is an offshoot of hypnosis, very rapidly gained ground.

In Britain with good reason – for wasn't James Braid an Englishman? – hypnosis achieved popularity in record time. From 1955 onwards it became a subject for study in medical school.

Medical applications of hypnosis are equally common in the United States where it has been officially recognised since 1958. Taught in medical school, its practice has a relevance in the treatment of all psychosomatic illnesses, but it is used in surgery as well, so that, depending on the case, either less anaesthetic or even none at all can be administered.

In the Soviet Union, even as early as the 1920s, far from putting a brake on its use, official medical circles encouraged research into hypnosis, and quickly engendered confidence in it, especially in the treatment of asthma, high blood pressure, duodenal ulcers, problems connected with the lining of the intestines and so on. Doctors in the Soviet

Union were also the first to introduce techniques derived from hypnosis into childbirth (painless childbirth).

In Germany as well, and in Central Europe, Scandinavia, and to a small degree everywhere else, hypnosis 'broke through' early this century, to remain a helpful adjunct to modern medicine.

The Rise of Self-hypnosis

Among the modifications and improvements which have taken place in the techniques of hypnosis during the last few hundred years, some point to the fact that the success of the treatment has been considerably helped by the patient's own contribution, by the practice of 'hypnotising oneself', sometimes at the moment of inducing the hypnosis, sometimes afterwards as well or just afterwards alone, or throughout the length of the treatment. Here are the main instances:

- At the time of hypnotising, instead of saying to the patient that he will have no choice but to experience such and such a sensation, he is asked to imagine or to acquire the conviction that he is experiencing a sensation of heat, relaxation, etc.
- When the hypnosis is complete, the hypnotist invites the patient (using the device known as 'posthypnotic suggestion') to use later on, when he is in an awakened state, a cue word (or coded word) which will make him re-experience the sensation of well-being he felt during the hypnosis session, or reaffirm his resolution (induced through hypnosis) to combat the sickness, pain or harmful addiction.

- To activate the cure, under medical control, the patient treats himself at home, using a hypnotic technique and following precise instructions on a tape-recording made specifically for him.
- If the patient can be hypnotised only with difficulty, he practises suitable hypnotic exercises at home which will lower his resistance to the therapy at the next session of hypnosis.

If the first of these methods sounds more like auto-suggestion, you will notice that the others employ real self-hypnotic techniques.

Characteristics in common

Self-hypnosis has developed very much along the lines of hypnosis, notably by adopting its fundamental characteristic of creating a special state, about halfway between waking and sleeping.

But it is not only in their effect on the mind, by which they create a detachment from immediate reality similar to the detachment found in sleep, that the two methods share common ground.

Like hypnosis, self-hypnosis has the advantage, on the one hand, of promoting a healthy state of total relaxation, and on the other, of mobilising 'undreamt-of energies' to bolster the individual's psychic resources that may be called upon to resolve a certain kind of problem.

These similarities explain why self-hypnosis, like hypnosis, is useful for:

- treating all psychosomatic illnesses, as well as various symptoms of impotence and frigidity that are of psychosomatic origin;
- combating pain, both as a method of anaesthesia in a surgical context and in other situations;
- a protection against stress;
- helping the individual in his studies, exams, pro-

fessional activities and competitive sports;
- promoting understanding between a couple, and also in a family context;
- easing the path of human relationships in general.

Just as its aims are similar to those of hypnosis, likewise there is no difference as regards their contra-indications: exactly as in the case of hypnosis, self-hypnosis is not formally recommended for psychotic patients or those with learning disabilities. (In addition, self-hypnosis is never recommended for those suffering from Stokes-Adam disease.)

How self-hypnosis differs from hypnosis

Apart from the fact that hypnosis takes place through the intervention of a specialist in the subject, while self-hypnosis can be practised without any very advanced study, the difference between the two methods exists purely and simply on a practical level, and is essentially this: self-hypnosis produces a kind of 'mini-hypnosis'.

This is why, since there is no risk of falling into a sleep which might prevent us pursuing our normal activities, we can call upon self-hypnosis not only when we are at home but also at work or indeed anywhere else.

The other difference is that self-hypnosis, on its own, can be successful only if the illness, sickness or other problem is not very serious, whereas hypnosis, whether backed up by self-hypnosis or not, can be successful even when the problem is severe.

The great leap

For thousands of years certain Eastern techniques (yoga, for example) have brought to the individual benefits similar to those achieved through self-hypnosis.

But if self-hypnosis has only belonged to this group of

relaxation methods for a relatively short time, that does not mean that it occupies only an insignificant position in the group. Quite the opposite is true: proof of its efficacy in the medical field has made it one of the prime methods used in complementary medicine, and this is one reason for its great leap in popularity. It is extremely useful for us today not only as a treatment but in the context of our daily life, no matter what the circumstances.

Techniques for Self-hypnosis and Similar Procedures

From very easy to more complex

Anyone can be hypnotised, providing he or she is willing. This means that unless there are any contra-indications (see p. 26), we can all practise self-hypnosis.

But, putting that consideration to one side for a moment, as well as such factors as the type of technique used and how competent the hypnotist is, it is a fact that the same individual can be easily hypnotised at one moment and cannot be at another.

In hypnosis, we rely on a 'trigger mechanism' which cannot be produced instantaneously every time. It is a phenomenon that can be observed in other areas of our psyche too, for example, sexual desire. Apart from the curious variation in the intensity of desire (depending on partner, physical circumstances and so on), there are instances when a man or woman who has for years been totally indifferent to the sexual attraction of someone he or she has met regularly as a friend or office colleague, quite suddenly falls head over heels for that person.

This trigger mechanism also plays a role in self-hypnosis. No matter what the technique used or how much experience you have had, sometimes the effect is immediate, sometimes there is a delayed reaction and sometimes it does not work at all.

Do not be discouraged if your first attempts are unproductive. If, on the other hand, you are successful right from the first when you embark on your exploration of this new field, do not presume that you always will be. Just as you cannot always forecast what sort of mood you are going to be in, or how dynamic you will feel from one moment to the next, it is, unfortunately, impossible to say how quickly self-hypnosis will take effect and give you the support you are looking for from it.

31

That said, let us now move on to describing some techniques that have proved their worth. Some are simply similar to those used in self-hypnosis (and familiarisation with them will help 'prepare the ground'), other techniques are a development from them.

1   The Navel Technique

When to use: for prevention of stress, mental and physical recovery, maintaining calm or restoring peace of mind.

This is a process derived from an ancient method of relaxation practised by the monks of Mount Athos in Greece.

Step-by-step guide

1   Find a quiet place and lie down on your back.
2   Close your eyes.
3   Breathe slowly, fully and deeply, with your stomach pushed out when you breathe in, and held in when you breathe out.
4   During this abdominal breathing, focus your mind's eye on your navel.
5   Set aside, totally, any thoughts that might come into your mind and continue to breathe as we have just described (with your stomach pushed out to breathe in, and held in to breathe out), without interrupting the contemplation of your navel . . .

Useful tips

Sometimes, you start feeling relaxed after only two or three minutes of exercise. If this is not the case, there is nothing wrong with starting again as many times as is necessary, saying to yourself, 'My feeling of relaxation comes from my navel.' People experienced in this technique just have to think of relaxing, as they concentrate on the mental picture of their navel.

2 The Third Eye Technique

When to use: as for Technique no. 1.

This is a process derived from one of the details in classic Eastern methods of concentration.

Step-by-step guide

1 For this exercise it does not matter whether you are lying on your back, standing or sitting, but close your eyes and begin to breathe from the stomach, with your stomach pushed out when you breathe in, and held in when you breathe out.

2 Look (in your imagination, obviously) at what the Tibetans call your third eye, that is to say, the tiny part of your skull which is just above the beginning of your nose, halfway between that and the top centre of your forehead, forming the apex of an imaginary triangle, of which the base angles are formed by the eyes.

3 Resist the temptation to pursue any thoughts that come into your mind; keep concentrating on your third eye, without ever interrupting your regular abdominal

breathing (if necessary, say in your mind: 'I am relaxing').

Useful tips

It is recommended that you persist with this exercise until you feel relaxed, but if nothing has happened after five to ten minutes, it would be better to try another technique.

3 The Tick-tock Technique

When to use: if peace of mind is only momentary, interrupted by vacillating thoughts giving rise to an irritability that interferes with study and professional work.

Here is a method (concentration on a regular sound) that often forms part of the one used by hypnotists, in the first stage of hypnotism.

Step-by-step guide

1   You can be standing, sitting or lying down. Concentrate all your attention on the tick-tocking of a watch, clock or metronome.
2   Allow yourself to be taken over by its uniform and regular sound, and say to yourself, 'There is nothing else but this.'
3   The moment you are aware that you have succeeded in blocking out everything but this sound, quickly close your ears for a few seconds.

Useful tip

It only takes a few minutes to achieve the desired effect.

4 The Total Void Technique

When to use: for anxiety and mild insomnia, but also the same symptoms as for Techniques 1, 2 and 3.

Here, the process involves the systematic wiping out of a specific mental picture.

Step-by-step guide

1   Whether you are standing, sitting or lying down (which, if you are fighting insomnia, would be essential), close your eyes.
2   Try to visualise, as precisely as you can, a familiar image, for example a certain room in your flat or house; say to yourself, 'For me, nothing else exists.'
3   Imagine in detail all the different elements that make up the picture in question (walls, floor, ceiling, windows, furniture, etc.).
4   One by one wipe the image of each of these elements from your mind, until you are left with absolutely nothing, total emptiness.
5   Stay like this, in the middle of this void, for a few

moments, so that you can experience the feeling of relaxation that will come from it.

Useful tips

If you are suffering from insomnia, and if the relaxed state still does not end in your falling asleep, you will have to do this exercise several times over. Otherwise, as a general rule, this method is usually successful after practising only a few minutes of 'disconnection'.

5   The Nostril Technique

When to use: to increase your ability to concentrate (should you have to carry out any sustained intellectual activity).

This process owes its effectiveness to the mobilisation of the respiratory system and to the relaxed state that ensues. It is generally performed either standing up or sitting.

Step-by-step guide

1   With fingers lightly spread, place your right hand over your navel and keep it there throughout the whole exercise.
2   Placing your left index finger in the middle of your forehead, block your left nostril with your left thumb, and breathe out through the right nostril, using abdominal breathing (with the stomach pushed out when breathing in, and your stomach held in when breathing out).
3   Breathe in slowly and deeply (with your stomach pushed out), concentrating your mind on the air that is entering through your right nostril alone (the left one still blocked by your left thumb).
4   After you have breathed in, close your right nostril

41

with the middle finger of your left hand.

5 Pause for a moment, with your lungs full.

6 With your stomach held in, breathe out slowly through the left nostril, after releasing the thumb that was blocking it and of course keeping the other nostril closed.

7 Pause for a few moments with your lungs empty.

8 Then breathe in through the left nostril, keeping your stomach pushed out.

9 After you have breathed in, close your left nostril, then repeat steps 2–8 ten times.

To sum up: whether it is the left or the right nostril, the procedure is the same: breathing out followed by breathing in.

Useful tips

While at first sight this exercise might give the impression of being rather complex, it actually takes less than one minute and can be learned in almost no time at all, but to begin with you must repeat it two or three times a day; then, after a week, you should practise it regularly once a day, telling yourself each time, 'I'm relaxing . . . I'm becoming more and more relaxed . . . I am completely relaxed.' Finally, when the technique has become virtually automatic, all you need do is say the word 'relaxed' in your head or out loud.

6 The Solar Plexus Technique

When to use: the same situations as for Technique no. 5.

Here again by combining imagination and breathing, you can achieve relaxation and thus enhance your capacity to concentrate.

Step-by-step guide

1 Place your fist (your left one if you are left-handed, right if you are right-handed) on your abdomen, above the navel.
2 Close your eyes.
3 Feel how, with the rhythm of your breathing, your hand is rising and falling in time with your abdomen.
4 Feel your solar plexus, that is to say, the area of your body against which your fist is presently resting, and imagine it in the shape of a small sun suspended in the hollow of your rib cage.
5 In your mind, go towards this sun. Using your imagination, make your brain 'descend' to the sun and unite with it.

6   Identify yourself totally with your solar plexus (the imaginary sun lodged within you); notice that all the energies in your body are converging towards this 'I' which is shining from the centre of your body.

7   Notice how the disordered jumble in your mind is fading (and with it, your fatigue).

8   Remain there in your mind, where you are, totally absorbed by this inner sun. Don't think of anything else except this precise point where your mental universe is fixed . . .

9   Once you have achieved absolute unity with the solar plexus and, through that, with the whole of your body, return towards your hand, which continues to rise and fall with the rhythm of your breathing.

10 Open your eyes.

Useful tips

It is advisable to repeat the exercise four times, over two days, until you master it. Then, so as not to lose your touch, practise it at least once a week, even outside the periods when you would use it to increase or consolidate your powers of concentration.

7   The Flame Technique

When to use: the same situations as for Techniques 5 and 6.

This exercise is one of the easiest, but it must be performed in a dark room and away from any distracting noises.

Step-by-step guide

1   Light a candle and switch off any other lights.
2   Sit yourself comfortably in an armchair, facing the candle.
3   Say to yourself: 'The candle flame will bring me inner peace.'
4   Don't think about anything, but let yourself relax as you contemplate the candle's flame.
5   Once you feel completely imbued with a sense of peace, close your eyes and relax your eyelids. At this moment, automatically, you will have the impression for a few seconds that you can see the flame. Whatever you do, don't lose this image. Do just the opposite, continue to watch it in your mind, until it disappears . . . a point which you have neither hastened nor delayed.
6   When the flame has faded from the screen of your imagination, make it reappear, but with your eyelids

45

still closed (in other words, imagine it there).

7   Stay like this, with your flame, for about thirty seconds.

Useful tip

During the first week you will need to spend time on this exercise every day. Afterwards you can repeat it once every three or four days.

8 The 'K' and 'S' Technique

When to use: as for Techniques 5, 6 and 7.

This is a method of relaxation derived from sophrological karate (developed by the author) in which this process plays an important role. This in turn derives from Technique no. 1.

Step-by-step guide

1 While either lying down or sitting, close your eyes.
2 Begin abdominal breathing (stomach pushed out for breathing in, stomach held in for breathing out).
3 Say to yourself: 'I am going to experience total detachment.'
4 Concentrate on your navel, imagine it and don't stop concentrating on it throughout the whole exercise.
5 Feel your navel rise when you breathe in and fall when you breathe out, saying all the time in your mind 'K' when you breathe in and 'S' when you breathe out.
6 Without worrying about the minutes passing, keep on visualising your navel and doing the abdominal

breathing, and always repeating in your mind 'K' when you breathe in and 'S' when you breathe out, until you experience the sensation of total detachment.

Useful tips

As a general rule, the feeling of total detachment will come after three or four minutes . . . provided you have succeeded in concentrating properly.

In order to master this technique (which is also helpful when your nerves are on edge), you must start by doing it between five and ten times, preferably once a day. Thereafter, it is advisable to practise it at least twice a week, so that it will work first time whenever you really need it.

9 The Storm Technique

When to use: when you are worried, anxious or apprehensive.

Here is a method that will progressively eliminate any unpleasant state caused through fear of one sort or another. It can also be used at times when you have feelings of anxiety, distress or fear for no apparent reason.

Step-by-step guide

1 Seat yourself as comfortably as possible in an arm-chair, or better still, lie down on a bed or sofa.
2 Close your eyes and stretch out your arms, then your legs.
3 Concentrate on your left hand and, one after the other, relax your fingers, beginning with the thumb.
4 When you have done that, do the same with your right hand.
5 In the same way, beginning with your big toe, relax your left foot, then your right foot.
6 Pause for a few moments and try not to think of anything, but breathe in and out deeply.
7 Imagine you are at the seaside or beside a lake and there is a storm. Imagine the waves stirred up by the wind.

8   With this image still in your mind, turn to look at the sky and let your eyes follow the movement of the clouds. Watch them come and go, with fewer and fewer of them in the sky, until a weak ray of sun appears on the far horizon which gradually becomes stronger and stronger . . .

9   Imagine the sky completely clear, then turn your attention to the surface of the water. In your mind, watch it become less and less agitated . . . until you see it completely smooth.

10 For two or three minutes, keep this image of the water, entirely calm and smooth, in your mind.

11 Breathe in and out deeply four or five times, without thinking of anything and keeping your eyes closed.

12 Think of the similarity between natural phenomena and the course of human existence, then say to yourself, 'Even if something painful must happen, in the end everything will work out for the best. I am like the water in the sea (or in the lake): after the disturbance that affected me, I am calm again, because there is absolutely no doubt that, sooner or later, things will get back to normal and order will be restored.'

13 Breathe in and breathe out deeply four or five times.

14 As at the beginning (step 2), stretch your arms, then your legs, and then say to yourself, 'I am calm, like the surface of the sea (or the lake) after the storm. I am going to stay calm. Nothing can take away my new-found serenity.'

15 Repeat aloud, or in your mind, whichever you like, 'I am calm,' several times, until you are sure you are, and can really sense the feeling of inner calm you so longed for.

Useful tips

Most often it only takes about ten minutes for this exercise to produce virtually instant results, especially if preceded by a relaxing bath.

10 The Punching Technique

When to use: fits of temper.

What could be more normal? Your patience, after all, has its limits, and it is not unusual for any of us to lose our temper when faced with some annoyance or injustice, spitefulness or malice. And then we get this overwhelming desire to punch the offending person in the face. But the prospect of the inevitable, unpleasant consequences deters us, obviously, from putting this into practice. We manage to stifle the overwhelming urge and, instead, give vent to our frustration or outrage in possibly quite hurtful invective. Our ill-temper arises from the fact that repressing our impulses releases our (sometimes innate) aggression and leaves us irritable, or fuming with rage for quite a while, with or without a violent headache.

So the exercise described below offers us a healthy means of releasing this feeling.

Step-by-step guide

1   Take the deepest breath you can, then breathe out very slowly.

2   Clench your fists as tightly as possible.

3   Preferably with your eyes closed (if circumstances permit) imagine you are in a boxing ring, in boxing gear, and that your opponent is the person who has made you so angry.

4   Breathe in and out rapidly. Each time you breathe out, expel the air forcefully, with your mouth slightly open. And at the same time, that is to say, every time you breathe out, clench your fists as tightly as possible, at the same time bringing them forward slightly (but not in an obvious way) and imagine you are punching your antagonist in the face.

5   Continue doing this in the way described in step 4, but saying silently to yourself: 'I'm getting my revenge, I'm hitting out, I'm hitting out. And every time I hit out, I'm releasing myself more and more from my anger. Every time I hit out, I feel more and more relaxed. Every time I hit out, I feel more and more relaxed and more and more tired.'

6   Imagine your adversary beginning to totter, then crumpling to the ground and that you, near to exhaustion, are watching him with the greatest satisfaction.

7   Breathe in and out slowly and deeply, three times, then say to yourself (always in your mind, of course), 'I've won. Now I'm extremely tired, but my anger has vanished. I'm relaxed. I'm calm.'

8   For several seconds, hold your breath and for the last time conjure up the image of your opponent stretched out on the floor of the ring. Savour the joy of this imaginary victory.

9   Breathe out hard and think, 'That's it. All my anger has gone. I'm calm, perfectly calm.'

10 Begin normal breathing again (and open your eyes, if you have had them closed since the beginning of the exercise).

Useful tips

The sole reason why I advise you to be careful to move your fists forward almost imperceptibly is that you may well be in the presence of the person who has provoked your anger. Otherwise, if you are alone and no one can see you, there is nothing to prevent you punching the air . . . or even thumping a cushion or some doll you can use as a whipping-boy.

Whatever the situation, so that you can develop this technique to its full for the appropriate moment, it is in your interest to practise it at first several times a day for a week. Then, when the day comes when you really need to use it, you will be able to rid yourself of your fit of aggression in less than a couple of minutes or so.

And if you are in a situation where you run the risk of losing your temper day after day (in the workplace or at home, or behind the steering wheel), I recommend you to begin each day with an exercise programmed to prevent this. It's simple: imagine the person who is likely to make you mad, and practise the technique of punching once or twice, according to how much time you have at your disposal. This will make you less susceptible when the person in question provokes an aggressive reaction in you.

Finally, make a note that this technique works best of all if you apply it at the very moment when you feel your rage coming on.

11 The Quicksand Technique

When to use: if you have a tendency to overeat.

Are you one of those men or women who have the ill-luck to put on weight all too easily? If the cause of this inconvenience can be attributed almost entirely to a sort of perpetually gargantuan appetite or excessive greediness, the quicksand technique may be able to help you.

Step-by-step guide

1 Find yourself a spot away from noise and in a semi-dark room.
2 Lie on your back and lie still. Relax for a few seconds or minutes; give yourself time to relax even if it is only for a short while.
3 If you have not already done so, close your eyes and breathe deeply, with your stomach pushed out when you breathe in and held in when you breathe out. Do this five or six times.
4 In order to stimulate the circulation of the blood to its proper level, keep moving your feet until you feel

them getting warm. At this stage, don't think any more about your breathing (in other words, you can breathe normally), but concentrate on the sensation of warmth in your feet.

5   Gently move your legs until they too feel warm. All the time you are doing this, imagine that the heat you are feeling in your feet is moving progressively up from your heels to your thighs.

6   Can you feel the warmth from your feet right up to your thighs? If you can, the moment has come for you to catapult yourself, in your imagination, into an exotic setting. Imagine that you are in the very middle of a virgin forest, buried up to the waist in a quicksand. Using your imagination, visualise two masked figures standing in front of you. One is dressed in white, the other in black. The one dressed in white is holding a stick out to you, so that you can grasp it and free yourself from the grip of the quicksand. The other figure (the one dressed in black) is holding out a plate filled with some of your favourite foods and, unfortunately, these are the very foods that are likely to make you fat.

7   You are faced with two choices. The first is for you to seize the stick. In this case you can conclude that your common sense has got the better of you and that you will be able to learn to conquer your bad habits and make the sacrifices necessary when you go on a slimming diet. If this is so, you have only to imagine that, because of the stick, everything will come right (far from sinking further into the quicksand, you will pull yourself out of it and be out of danger). Consequently, you will say to yourself: 'Just as I imagined I could when I was in the middle of the virgin forest, I will make myself able to resist temptation day after day. I will avoid (or limit) eating foods which make me fat. I will get slim (or at least I won't get any fatter) and I will get there. There is absolutely no doubt that I shall get there.'

Now look at the other option. If in your imagination you were automatically driven towards not choosing the stick but taking the plate and immediately eating its contents, only one conclusion can be drawn: if you want to slim (or not get any fatter), you will have to muster all your will-power and make a lot more effort. That is why, in this case, it is absolutely essential that you use self-hypnosis to put yourself in a bad situation. Yes, you must imagine that with each morsel of fattening food that you swallow, even if it is just the tiniest crumb, the quicksand is sucking you down more and more. But as soon as you stop eating one or other of your favourite foods, you begin to feel slightly less heavy and a strange force, coming from the bowels of the earth, lifts you out a little. After noticing this for a while, you manage to push the plate away, and resolve never to touch any of it again. Immediately, you rise completely out of the quicksand, as if by a miracle, without even needing the stick . . . Savour this sensation of new-found freedom and say to yourself: 'I have resolved to eat less (or to go without such and such a fattening food completely). Whenever I feel the urge to stuff myself, I am going to remember the image of the quicksand swallowing me up. I shall conquer my insatiable appetite (or my excessive greed) and I shall get thinner (or I shall not get any fatter). I refuse to stay (or become) fat. I have decided to make some sacrifices.'

8 Breathe out deeply and pull in your stomach as much as possible. Stay this way for several seconds, with your stomach drawn in as far as it will go, allowing the following idea to take you over: 'My intestines are shrinking . . . they are shrinking . . . And because they are shrinking, it will be easier for me to eat less (or not to eat any) of this or that.'

9 Practise this abdominal breathing four or five times (when you breathe in, push your stomach out; when you breathe out, pull your stomach in). Make sure that

every time you breathe out, you hold your stomach in as much as you possibly can. At the same time, imagine once more that you are being swallowed up by the quicksand, but that with each breath you expel, you are climbing out of it. And say to yourself: 'Every time I breathe out, I am losing weight, my stomach is getting less and less big. I am feeling good, I'm feeling lighter and lighter. And in order to go on enjoying this very pleasant sensation of lightness, I have decided to eat less of this or that (or go without them altogether).'

10   Open your eyes. Really stretch your arms and legs. Get up, repeating (aloud or in your mind): 'I have decided to eat less of this or that (or to go without them altogether).'

Useful tips

Once you have learned this technique by practising it several times, it is a good idea to do it every morning before breakfast, and every evening before dinner, at least initially. Then, when the effect begins to show, you can just do it once a day, preferably in the morning and always before eating. But independently of this, if you know you have to have a meal which threatens your diet (in a restaurant or at some friends' or your parents'), it would be wise to fit in an additional exercise about one hour before the big feed-up.

All that remains to be said is this: it is not always easy to fight overweight just by using self-hypnosis. You must also scrupulously follow the rules of the diet, and never neglect any medical advice.

12 The Ascent in a Balloon Technique

When to use: after suffering various setbacks.

This technique is particularly suited to very sensitive people, those who, after a setback, seem unable to make a fresh start, and who feel so shaken that they go on torturing themselves by reliving the memory of what shocked, deceived, disturbed or horrified them in the first place.

The aim is to achieve a state of detachment, which will allow them to see the cause of their emotional chaos in perspective.

Step-by-step guide

1 Sit yourself down, but in such a way that your feet are not touching the ground, and preferably in a place undisturbed by noise.

2 Close your eyes and breathe regularly, breathing in and out as deeply as possible.

3 Imagine that you are aboard a balloon (like an old-fashioned hot-air balloon or a more modern aerostat), and that each time you breathe out, this balloon ascends

higher and higher above the house, the neighbourhood, then the town or village where you live.

4   Without interrupting your regular breathing (taking the deepest possible breaths), say to yourself: 'I am growing lighter, lighter and lighter . . . And the lighter I become, the further the balloon is from the ground.'

5   After a minute or two, imagine that you have reached a considerable height: houses, trees, cars and so on appear tiny, and spread out below the balloon that is carrying you higher and higher, the visible surface of the earth is shrinking more and more.

6   Let yourself savour this wonderful feeling of lightness (in the end it is intoxicating) and enjoy the sense of relaxation that comes with this feeling.

7   Imagine that you continue your ascent, until you can look down and see the whole globe, just as if you were an astronaut – that is to say, you can see it reduced to the size of a small ball.

8   In your imagination, try to visualise, like one of these far-off observers, the scene of the event that upset you (or was the cause of your disappointment, anxiety or horror), and say to yourself: 'All this is a long way away, a really long way . . . Thousands of miles separate me from the place where this horrid thing happened . . . I am feeling good, I feel happy and relaxed, nothing can upset me.'

9   After taking a deep breath, hold it and repeat in your mind, 'I feel good, I feel relaxed and happy, nothing can upset me.'

10 Then return to your normal breathing and open your eyes.

Useful tips

The number of times you will need to do this exercise varies. You must take into account not only the nature and seriousness of the trauma you have undergone, but also your own degree of sensitivity. No matter whether it is of equal or similar importance (for example, a quarrel with a loved one or the arrival of an unexpectedly high tax demand), some people succeed in overcoming their anxiety after practising the technique two or three times or even only once, whereas others need to do the exercise several times a day for a week or two, before being able to set aside totally (or even partially) whatever it was that upset them so terribly.

13   The Wheel of Fortune Technique

When to use: an episode of bad luck.

It is a commonplace to say that life is full of ups and downs. No one can escape it. But while some people can accept misfortune with stoicism, even if ill-luck dogs them for several weeks, months or years, others risk drowning in despair at the very first whiff of any type of catastrophe.

But . . . provided it is practised conscientiously, this technique, known as the Wheel of Fortune (after the tenth arcana in the *Tarot*) can help enormously in regaining the necessary courage to continue the struggle for life.

Step-by-step guide

1   Find a quiet place in a room where no one will come to disturb you.
2   Sit in the lotus position with your legs crossed, and place your hands on your knees.
3   Close your eyes, and breathe abdominally (push your stomach out when you breathe in and hold your stomach in when you breathe out). Do this for as long

as it takes to relax. To do it properly, concentrate on the in-and-out movement of your stomach, so that it will be easier to empty yourself of every thought (especially thoughts connected with the latest problem or whole host of problems you have encountered).

4   Once you have become detached from the problems that were preoccupying you, imagine an amusement park, and take up a position on a platform far away from the crowd, where you can calmly contemplate the Big Wheel.

5   Start to breathe normally (in other words without needing to observe how you perform your abdominal breathing) and, following the motion of the Big Wheel, as you visualise it in your imagination, begin slowly to rotate your head, exactly as if you were doing a gymnastic exercise to loosen up the cervical vertebrae.

6   Continue rotating your head slowly and without pause. In your thoughts, identify yourself with the Big Wheel, which is turning, turning and sometimes takes the passengers right up in the air, and sometimes brings them right down to the ground . . .

7   Say to yourself, either aloud or in your head, but you must synchronise the words with the movement of your chin going either up or down: 'I'm going up . . . up . . . I'm going down . . . down . . .'

8   Do your best to be aware of the feeling of calm, of detachment or even serenity that the uninterrupted movement has created in you. Savour these moments of peace to the full.

9   Again, either out loud or in your head, it doesn't matter, say to yourself: 'I am calm, detached, serene. It doesn't matter whether I go up or down, it's the same, I am calm, detached, serene . . .' (If necessary, repeat these phrases several times until you have made yourself believe absolutely in what you are saying.)

10   Stop rotating your head, take a deep breath, then hold it for a few moments, giving yourself enough time to

remember the Big Wheel that you have conjured up in your imagination.

11   Begin breathing normally again and say to yourself: 'I swear never to despair ever again. I now understand that every descent is bound to be followed by an ascent. I now understand that my trial has come to an end. That it could not be otherwise. My descent will soon be followed by ascent. Misfortune will be nothing more than a bad memory. My good luck will return. Although I was down, I shall be going up again, and I am on the way up.'

12   Open your eyes, stand up, then stretch as you breathe in with full lungs and repeat in your head your solemn undertaking: 'I am not going to despair. I know my next chance of good luck is just around the corner.'

Useful tips

The tenth arcana of the *Tarot*, the Wheel of Fortune, is illustrated by a big wheel with a handle (the sort you can see at a fairground, and dating from the Middle Ages). Seated on it is a demonic figure with wings and a crown, symbols of strength, power and riches. To his left, caught on the wheel, is another person of demonic appearance, in the act of going down, while a third demon on the right is being carried upwards by the wheel. As in other divinatory cards with similar illustrations, this card suggests the idea of the hazards of fortune; it reminds us that human existence corresponds to an uninterrupted succession of periods of good and bad luck. This is why our Technique no. 13 refers to it . . .

    As to the number of exercises that need to be performed, this again depends on the individual, as well as the gravity of his or her situation, and the size of the catastrophe. If there is no shortage of people who can be up and fighting again after a few days, after only three or four daily exercises, there are also those – and quite a few of them – who need to persevere for at least ten days or so, with five or six exercises a day. In all these cases, the most important thing is not to give up, but to persist until you can convince yourself of the meaning of hope: that there are better days to come.

14 The 'Cosmic Battery' Technique

When to use: for shyness or timidity.

It is true that for many people shyness is a characteristic that goes right back to their childhood. But very often it can also be due to a series of setbacks, or can be the result of bad luck in a professional situation or in matters of love (or sometimes both at once), and many people end up losing the self-confidence they had, either entirely or in part. So much so that, when the day comes when they have the opportunity to forge ahead, instead of being able to take advantage of it, they act in a way that deprives them of any chance of success . . . or they dare not act at all. This handicap sometimes shows itself, for example, at an important interview which is crucial to the development of their career (either for a new job or promotion) or when they meet a person who seems to be the ideal one to put an end to all their loneliness.

Here, then, is a technique that has been worked out as much for those suffering from innate shyness, as for those who have lost their confidence as a result of certain events.

Step-by-step guide

1   If you can, go outside into the open air, or find a quiet, airy room, and lie down on your back.

2   Lie with your arms by your sides so that the backs of your hands are touching the ground and your legs are stretched out in front of you, so that your heels are firmly on the ground and the soles of your feet are turned slightly upwards.

3   Close your eyes and breathe deeply, forcing yourself to clear your mind of any specific thoughts.

4   After a few seconds or minutes, or in other words, at the moment when your thoughts stop madly racing, stretch out further and let yourself be filled with a feeling of relaxation.

5   Practise abdominal breathing scrupulously (push your stomach out as you breathe in, and pull it back as you breathe out). Do this about ten times.

6   If you are doing this exercise out of doors, open your eyes and look at the sky. If you are indoors, keep your eyes closed and contemplate the celestial vault in your mind, imagining it full of sunlight or strewn with stars, according to whether it is day or night.

7   Think about the innumerable multitude of stars in the universe and the unquestionable influence that the sun, moon and planets of our solar system in general exert throughout the world.

8   Spread your fingers (with your palms still facing upwards) and spread out your toes (with the soles of your feet still turned up) and imagine that from that very moment your hands and feet are 'antennae that will capture the energy of the universe'.

9   Resume your abdominal breathing and imagine that each intake of breath is a dose of cosmic energy entering right into your body, which thus becomes a 'cosmic battery'.

10   Say to yourself: 'I am recharging myself with energy . . .

With every breath I take, my potential for energy is growing . . . With every breath I take, I am becoming stronger, more powerful, more courageous. With every breath I take, I am becoming more and more conscious of the reality of my strength, power, and courage . . . With every breath I take, I am discarding more and more of my shyness . . . I feel strong, powerful and full of courage, I am perfectly conscious of the fact that I have nothing to envy in others.'

11 At this stage, as a rule, you are sure to experience a sensation not only of well-being, but also of a sudden great surge of vitality. Breathe even deeper and try to be aware of all the energy bringing your body to life.

12 Either in your head or aloud, say to yourself: 'With a recharged battery like this, my body has accumulated an enormous quantity of energy . . . I am aware of the huge extent of my mental and physical capacities . . . I am aware of the silliness of my shyness and timidity . . . I know that the energies accumulated within me will give me the strength to face any situation, come what may . . . I know that I shall never be throttled by shyness again . . . Whether at work or in my private life, whatever the occasion, I will always be capable of acting or reacting with complete self-confidence.'

13 With your legs and arms still stretched out (as at the beginning of the exercise), bring your hands together, palm to palm, and your feet, left big toe to right big toe, left heel to right heel; then imagine that, like a gushing torrent, all this surplus energy accumulated in you is now circulating freely in your body, all along your legs, your torso and arms.

14 Repeat to yourself: 'My body is like a completely recharged battery . . . My body is like a completely recharged battery . . . I am overflowing with energy . . .'

15 If you have your eyes closed, open them, stand up and stretch up on tiptoe with your arms raised, breathing

deeply and, at the moment of breathing out, say aloud to yourself: 'I am overflowing with energy, my shyness no longer exists.'

15a If possible, and if there are no medical reasons against it, you can now take a hot shower followed by a cold one, so that you can experience the dynamism that has developed inside you.

To increase the impact of your resolve not to be restrained or blocked by shyness ever again, you can 'demystify' the point at which other people might arouse your sense of shyness and timidity: imagine them naked and in the act of doing what every human being needs to do at least once a day . . .

Useful tips

If your shyness is very deeply ingrained and tends to surface in every type of situation, you must do this exercise at least twice a day (the first time in the morning, preferably), for three or four weeks, as required. But if you are likely to feel timid only in certain circumstances or only in the presence of certain people (those higher in the hierarchy, for example), quite often you will only need to do this for a week or ten days, twice a day, to acquire a self-confidence that will surprise your colleagues.

15 The Mirror Technique

When to use: for male sexual problems.

Note: this is not a remedy for impotence in the proper sense of the word, since that can only be treated successfully using hypnotherapy . . . and provided it has a psychosomatic cause.

On the other hand, practising the exercise described below will give excellent results if you want to prevent the repetition of certain mishaps, which most often occur either as a result of nothing more than habit, or because of financial or other worries, or are due to some kind of complex (which triggers off a feeling of apprehension about failure or partial failure).

Step-by-step guide

1   Go to a room that is quiet, and either sit comfortably or lie down; close your eyes, relax, breathe in a regular rhythm and try not to think about anything.
2   When you have succeeded in ridding yourself of all your thoughts, continue your regular breathing, but breathe in and out as deeply as you can, about ten times.
3   Think about the love-making you are likely to have,

and with each intake of breath, imagine that the air you have breathed in is going straight to your penis, and that this air will make it feel warm.

4 Say to yourself: 'The more I breathe in, the warmer my penis will become . . . The more I breathe in, the more likely that my penis will have an erection, just as it does in my warm bed some mornings (or every morning) . . . The more I breathe in, the warmer my penis will be.'

5 Try to recall one of your more brilliant sexual performances and say to yourself: 'There's no reason at all why this should be just a memory . . . It can be reproduced. It will be the same next time. I'll make love fantastically well again.'

6 Using the power of your imagination, project yourself into the near future. Imagine you are there with your partner whom you have met somewhere, or who has come to your home or wherever you have arranged to meet. But, when you visualise the scene, imagine that, this time, you are making love in front of a mirror and you can see yourself in the act of making love, as if you were present at someone else's love-making.

7 Still using the power of your imagination, admire this superman (you), who is making love with such amazing skill and momentum, making her moan and cry out with pleasure, and moving from one position to another without the slightest hesitation.

8 Say to yourself: 'That's how it's going to be. I shall be impetuous, tireless, sublime.' Then, depending on your own situation or circumstances, add:

a 'I shall be erect right from the start' (if, to get an erection, you normally need your partner to stimulate you manually or orally);

b 'I can take all the time in the world' (if you suffer from premature ejaculation);

c 'I shall be in a permanent state of erection' (if, sometimes, or often, your erection goes limp or vanishes altogether);

d 'I shall come easily' (if, as a matter of course, or only now and then, in order to reach an orgasm you have to force yourself, or resort to fantasies – for example, imagining that the person beside you is someone else).

9 Linger over this imagined erotic scene. Then, so that you totally convince yourself, repeat this to yourself, either in your head or out loud: 'This is how it's going to be.' And each time, add one or other of the sentences in a, b, c, or d, whichever applies to you.

10 Breathe in and out deeply, then open your eyes and stand up, with your mind at ease, reassured that you are perfectly capable of not disappointing your partner.

Useful tips

Let us return to the cause of the problems. Of course, it is said that technical defects occur most frequently as a result of habit, worry or some complex (whether or not due to previous failures). But it would be wrong to underestimate the importance of physical condition. In fact, one's worst enemy in this situation is tiredness. On its own or even more likely if coupled with one of the classic obstacles cited (habit, worries, complexes), it erects a barrier which is difficult to surmount. This is why, when it is a question of physical tiredness, it is better to agree to some rest and relaxation (for example, using the self-hypnosis technique described in Technique no. 19) before embarking on sexual activity. And if, in addition to ridding yourself of physical tiredness, you also use the Mirror Technique as a precaution, then one hopes that you will not have any of these problems.

That said, the exercise that has just been described is most helpful if, after you have learned it, you practise it no earlier than one or two hours before love-making takes place. The ideal time to do it would be just a few minutes before you go into action.

16   The Niagara Falls Technique

When to use: for female sexual problems.

As with the preceding technique, this one does not claim to be able to eliminate or alleviate major difficulties in cases of true frigidity. Quite modestly, it promises moments of intense pleasure (or even ecstasy) only to women who do not always feel particularly predisposed to give themselves to their partner, and/or only reach orgasm with great difficulty.

So the following exercise will be of use only to those women whose 'sexual appetite' is in no way diminished, or has been stifled because of some powerful psychological trauma, or after illness or surgery.

Step-by-step guide

1   Preferably have a bath first, then go to a room where you can be left in peace and quiet. Make sure there is plenty of air, and that the room is only dimly lit. Then make yourself comfortable and take off anything tight: shoes, bra, pants and watch. Lie down on your back.

72

2 Fix your gaze on the standard lamp or a precise point on the ceiling, and begin breathing deeply, with your stomach out when you breathe in and held in when you breathe out.

3 Continue with this abdominal breathing, keeping your eyes firmly on the lamp or point on the ceiling, and keep this up until you start feeling tired.

4 Close your eyes and stretch out, give a long sigh and begin to breathe normally, that is to say, without having to watch how regularly or how deeply you are breathing. Try to think of nothing, relax, relax . . .

5 Once you feel well and truly relaxed, imagine you are on holiday. It doesn't matter where. In the United States, perhaps, or, to be more precise, at the Niagara Falls. Yes, in your imagination, admire this most famous waterfall in the world, and go on to imagine that you are breathing air that is exceptionally rich in ozone, air that is purifying your blood and your whole body.

6 Begin breathing to a regular rhythm (abdominally, or otherwise, whichever you prefer), ensuring that you breathe as deeply as you possibly can. And say to yourself: 'With each intake of breath, my blood and my whole body are becoming purer and purer . . . With each intake of breath, I am becoming more and more relaxed and capable of having sex (or making love, if you feel that term is more appropriate) . . . With each intake of breath, I am feeling better and better and more and more willing to be fondled, kissed, penetrated . . . With each intake of breath, I feel more and more ready to indulge in the pleasures of sex . . . With each intake of breath, I am becoming more and more able to forget my worries, my apprehensiveness, the rambling thoughts preventing me from having numerous orgasms or even just one . . . With each intake of breath, my desire, my desire to come is growing.'

7   If, in the course of step 6, the image of the Niagara Falls has dimmed, or even disappeared, bring it back into focus. But if the famous waterfall has not left the screen in your mind, go on to say to yourself immediately, either in your head or out loud: 'I am not going to let either tiredness or upsets or anything whatsoever deprive me of a perfect sexual understanding with my partner (if this is not the case, you can add, '. . . even if he doesn't do exactly what I would like him to) . . . Nothing will stop me from feeling pleasure and coming.'

8   Take a deep breath and hold it for several seconds, long enough to imagine yourself in the throes of an orgasm, then breathe out deeply and repeat (this time you must say it aloud): 'Nothing will stop me from feeling pleasure and coming.'

8a If ever you are still not optimistic enough about your future ability to have the desired reactions (to the point of being able to reach orgasm) you must return in your imagination to the Niagara Falls, and practise step 6 of the exercise again, and if need be, do this several times one after the other, until you can shake off your pessimism.

9   Put your hand on your sex, press it lightly and promise yourself one last time, still out loud: 'Nothing will stop me from feeling pleasure and coming.'

10 Open your eyes and get up.

Useful tips

Many men are unaware that women take longer to become sexually aroused than they do. That is why I am going to ask you this indiscreet question: does your partner belong to this category? If he does, then you must make up your mind, as a priority, to enlighten him: explain to him, among other details, where your particularly erogenous zones are, and don't hesitate either to tell him that you cannot manage without foreplay, which must be done in such and such a way. Without that, even the most conscientious and most frequent practice of this exercise may well remain useless . . .

It remains to be said that, as in Technique no. 15, it would be a good idea to carry out this exercise just before making love (after, of course, learning it properly). Apart from this, just at the beginning or even during sex, it can be useful in consolidating the resolution you made under self-hypnosis. How? By doing step 9 of the exercise. (Usually, the partner is delighted and excited as well when he sees the woman touching herself, and hears her say that she intends to have at least one orgasm, if not more.)

17 The Net Technique

When to use: for impatience.

Let us stay in the field of sexuality for a moment and draw attention to another frequent cause of male failure: impatience. How many times does a man, in far too great a hurry in his desire to penetrate, become a victim to nerves, bringing his means to an abrupt end, or a partial end anyway! Or, by showing excessive impatience, he makes his partner non-receptive or even openly hostile, so much so that, as a reaction, his fighting spirit flags and he ends up in a degrading situation with a wilting erection or premature ejaculation . . .

But impatience can be equally prejudicial in a professional and/or social setting. As an example, you have only to think of motorists who end up getting a thrashing, or are sometimes accidentally beaten to death by other drivers, for the simple reason that they were unlucky enough to trumpet their impatience too noisily in a traffic jam or some similar hold-up. Fortunately self-hypnosis can act like a protective shield for those who take the trouble to learn it.

Step-by-step guide

1 Sit in a comfortable armchair away from noise and strong light.

2 Stretch your legs, straighten your arms, spread your fingers slightly, close your eyes and relax. Breathe to a regular rhythm, and try not to think about anything.

3 Enjoy this feeling of relaxation for a few minutes, then imagine that you are in a forest, about to go down a path. All around you, everything is pleasant and reassuring. There is no sign of any danger to put you on the alert.

4 Practise abdominal breathing (with your stomach pushed out when you breathe in and held in when you breathe out). Do this ten times, while continuing your imaginary walk through the forest.

5 After you have breathed out deeply, imagine that, all of a sudden, you walk right into a big net for catching game and you are trapped . . . Not unnaturally, with your usual impatience you struggle against it, trying to free yourself as quickly as you can. But the more you struggle, the more the net wraps itself around you, exactly as if you were a fly in a web.

6 In your imagination, it goes without saying, stop struggling and stay still under the net, then say to yourself: 'I must keep calm . . . I must keep calm . . . If I want to get out, I must stay calm. I shall only be able to get out if I stay calm . . .'

7 Return to your abdominal breathing and continue imagining that you are under the net. Say to yourself: 'I am getting calmer and calmer . . . With each intake of breath, I am becoming more and more able to be patient. And the more patient I become, the easier it will be for me to find a way of escaping.'

8 After you have practised your abdominal breathing in this way for two or three minutes, breathe out as deeply as you can, then hold your breath and say to

yourself: 'At this moment I am completely calm . . . At this moment I can prove that I am patient . . . And by being patient I shall be able to get out of this.'

9 Continue to hold your breath and imagine that, very gently, steadily, you manage to unravel the net that is wound around you, until you reach a point where you can remove it completely.

10 Take a deep breath and resume your normal breathing pattern. Say to yourself: 'I've done it. I am free. I am free again because I was patient.'

11 Continue your imaginary walk through the forest and say to yourself: 'I am not afraid of anything. If something like that happens again, I know how to get out of the net. With patience, I shall be able to free myself. And the same will happen in other situations. Whatever happens at home, at work or anywhere else, I shall always react patiently.'

12 Hold your breath one last time, for as long as you possibly can; then, before opening your eyes and getting up, promise yourself: 'No matter what happens, just as I was able to hold my breath at that moment, I shall always be able to exercise self-control and not lose patience.'

Useful tips

Parodoxically, you need a lot of patience to overcome your impatience. The obstacles, however, are not insurmountable. With will-power, you can, for the price of three exercises a day for a week or ten days, already make great progress. Afterwards, if you want to conquer your impatience, both men and women with determination need only one exercise a day, preferably in the morning.

18　The Automatic Writing Technique

When to use: during a period of grieving, and if you fear death.

In the testing period after a much-loved person has died, self-hypnosis can offer consolation, help you come to terms with your loss, lessen the pain or overcome it. This is achieved by a self-hypnotic process that has been in use for a hundred years or more and is still practised in spiritualist circles throughout the world.

This process helps to convince you of the reality of life after death – that is to say, the reality of the immortality of the spirit, temporarily lodged in each human body. The technique works on the premise that it is possible to enter into contact with the dead. And it can be used not only during a period of mourning, but also at those times when, because of a serious illness or for some other reason, you may feel terrified at the idea of reaching the end of your own life.

Step-by-step guide

1　Take steps to ensure that you will not be disturbed,

then shut yourself away in a quiet room, lit only by a candle.

2   In front of you, place one or more sheets of blank paper, as well as the photograph of the beloved person whose spirit you wish to contact, then try to remember that person as intensely as you can.

3   Imagine that this person, even if invisible, is close to you, and talk to him or her. Depending on how you feel, ask him or her either to dispel your fears about death, or help you through this testing period which weighs so heavily upon you after his or her death. (You can ask this aloud, or only in your mind, whichever you wish.)

4   Pick up a pencil or pen and hold it over the sheet of paper, exactly as if you were preparing to write a letter.

5   Fix your eyes intently on the flame of the candle and, without thinking of anything specific, breathe in a regular rhythm, but as deeply as you possibly can.

6   Don't worry about time passing, don't get impatient, fix your eyes on the candle and breathe deeply . . . until you have the impression that your hand holding the pencil or pen is beginning to move.

7   Close your eyes and force any specific thoughts out of your mind. The screen in your brain must be completely blank. You must forget, ignore the reality of your hand holding the pencil or pen. It is essential that your hand moves without the slightest influence of your will.

8   If you notice that the paper has been filled and that your hand is still writing in the air or directly on the surface of the table you are sitting at, with your free hand slip another sheet of paper under the hand guided by the spirit. Having done that, close your eyes. With deep, regular breathing and your mind free of any thought, once again submerge yourself completely in the self-hypnotic state which allowed you to

begin and will allow you to continue what is known as automatic writing.

8a If you notice that your hand holding the pencil or pen is no longer moving, open your eyes and consider the experience finished. All you need to do now is examine the sheet or sheets of paper. In the best hypothetical scenario, you will be able to read entire words and sentences in a very clear reply to your question. Very often, however, the message obtained can be delphic. It is then up to you to undertake the (not easy) task of deciphering it.

(Let me give you an example. Suppose you had asked for some sort of comfort after the early death of someone very close. But, instead of 'I'm happy in the afterlife' or 'My spirit stays close to you' or 'Don't torment yourself any longer', you may, quite simply, read the word 'Sun'. This could be an allusion to the happiness that awaits you when you have breathed your last, or it could be advice to accept philosophically the tragic event that occurred and continue to live with the sun in your soul . . . Clearly, in this case, there has been no problem in working out the possible meaning. The annoying thing is that for most of the time, the interpretation of the message which at first sight seems incomprehensible requires a lot of effort.) Finally, in the worst of hypothetical situations, the paper is completely covered with scribbles devoid of any meaning at all.

Useful tips

There is absolutely no guarantee that your efforts will be crowned with success right from the word go. But you should not be discouraged by an unsuccessful outcome. The next day or the day after that, there is nothing to stop you from trying again. The result depends very much on your powers of concentration (steps 2 and 3), then on how completely you relax (steps 5, 6 and 7), and it goes without saying that some days you will not be sufficiently on form to concentrate, or to relax comfortably.

One thing is certain: it is a universally known fact, thanks to the work of the Breton, Allan Kardec, and endorsed by another master of spiritualism, Sir Arthur Conan Doyle, that automatic writing has proved and continues to prove its efficacy. Apart from the importance of its role in the literary field (many famous writers both past and present have confirmed that, using it as a medium, authors who have been excised from the book of the living can express themselves through automatic writing and in the works of those who practise it), it is, above all, a way of strengthening or renewing the hope of finding again those who have left us only in their physical guise.

19   The Black Fishes Technique

When to use: for fatigue, to boost energy.

This procedure is ideal as an antidote to momentary tiredness, when you suddenly feel whacked. It can, in addition,
increase your vitality, but only if you enjoy bathing and
water and see them as a tonic, something that gives you a
feeling of well-being. (In other words, if you have a horror
of water, this won't be for you.)

Step-by-step guide

1   You can sit, lie down or stand up for this exercise.
Close your eyes.
2   Say to yourself: 'I am going to overcome my tiredness,'
or, 'I am going to increase my vitality many times
over,' whichever is relevant to your particular case.
3   Visualise a river (or a lake or swimming-pool) with
limpid water that makes you feel you want to plunge
straight in.
4   Using the magic of your imagination, dive in and feel
your tiredness drifting away like a shoal of thousands

of tiny black fishes, swimming farther and farther away.

Or if you want to increase your vitality, imagine that contact with the water mobilises your energy, more and more . . .

5   When the 'tired fish' have disappeared, breathe deeply and let yourself float, completely relaxed.

If you are using this technique to become more dynamic, imagine your energy catapulting you to the surface of the water, then savour the relaxing feeling of being spread out on the surface.

6   Stretch as much as you can (to get rid of the last vestiges of tension, or to accentuate the feeling that you are full of energy). Don't just imagine you are doing this but do it in reality too, stretching especially your neck, arms and legs . . .

7   Imagine that you are sinking like a stone to the bottom of the river (or lake or swimming-pool) and feel the water's pleasant caress as, in your imagination, it surrounds you on all sides.

8   Rise up to the surface, bringing yourself back to the real world.

9   Breathe out, then breathe in deeply.

10   Enjoy the sense of relaxation you feel, and pay close attention to the rhythm of your breathing: feel the air going into your lungs and feel the air you are expelling.

11   Open your eyes.

Useful tip

This exercise can also be practised as a preventive measure (to avoid fatigue, and to keep feeling fit), at least once a day, preferably in the morning.

20 The Thousand Suns Technique

When to use: as for Technique no. 19.

This exercise works better if you are already relaxed from the start, so you may first need to practise one of the techniques described earlier, such as nos. 1, 2 or 3.

Step-by-step guide

1 You may sit down for this, but sit up straight.
2 Close your eyes and say to yourself: 'I am going to get rid of my tiredness,' or, 'I am going to increase my vitality many times over.'
3 Pushing out your stomach, take a deep, slow breath, and imagine that the air you are breathing in is spangled with a thousand tiny suns (symbols of energy).
4 Hold your breath and concentrate on your feet: think of nothing but them; imagine that they are surrounded, blanketed and pierced by a swarm of tiny suns.
5 Breathe out, and imagine that, along with the expelled air, you are also expelling thousands of bits of rubbish

from your body, and that the air you are breathing out is stale and grey.

6 Pause for a while in your breathing.

7 Take another slow, deep breath, with your stomach pushed out, and again imagine that the air you are breathing in is thronging with a host of tiny suns.

8 Hold your breath and concentrate on your legs. Think of nothing except your legs, and imagine them surrounded, blanketed and pierced by millions of tiny suns.

9 Breathe out, as described above in step 5.

10 Pause for a few moments without breathing.

11 With your stomach pushed out, breathe in, slowly and deeply, and continue to imagine that the air you are breathing in is full of tiny suns.

12 Hold your breath and concentrate on your thighs, visualising the tiny suns now reaching up to them.

13 Breathe out slowly, very slowly, still imagining that the breath you expel is purifying your body.

14 Wait for several seconds without breathing.

15 Open your eyes and begin breathing normally again.

Once you are familiar with this procedure (some manage it right from the beginning, others need to practise it five to ten times before they get it right), you can go on to the second stage, concentrating in turn, at the moment when you hold your breath (steps 4, 8 and 12), on:

● the upper part of the abdomen;
● the hollow of the stomach (solar plexus);
● the chest.

After you have properly assimilated this second stage, begin the third, concentrating in turn, at the moment when you hold your breath (steps 4, 8 and 12), on:

● the hands;
● the forearms;

- the whole of your arms;
- the shoulders.

Having mastered the third stage, proceed to the fourth, concentrating in turn, at the moment when you hold your breath, on:

- the jaws;
- the eyes;
- the throat.

Finally, when you have learned to do this fourth stage, move on to the fifth and final one, concentrating in turn, as you hold your breath (steps 4, 8 and 12), on:

- the spinal column;
- the back of your head;
- the front part of your head.

Useful tips

Once you have learned all five stages of this technique, you can practise the whole exercise at a single sitting and, if you want to be on good form every day, ideally it should be done daily; otherwise you can do it just when you feel a need to revitalise your nervous system, or to fill your body with energy – in other words, every time you feel it necessary to inject some vitality into your system.

21 The Breath Technique

When to use: to strengthen the nervous system in order to prevent stress.

This technique, originating in the East, works by combining the power of the imagination with the activation of your respiratory system to provide special protection from the ill-effects of noise and other factors that can cause stress.

Step-by-step guide

1 Lie comfortably on your back, preferably in a dark or dimly lit room, as far from noise as possible.
2 Close your eyes and say to yourself: 'I am going to be calm . . . I am going to be more and more calm . . . completely calm.'
3 Breathe in with your stomach out, and breathe out with your stomach in, three times. Do this very gently, and hold your breath for a few moments between each intake and expulsion of breath, and also between each expulsion and intake of breath.
4 When you breathe out for the third time, direct your breath to your toes and relax them.

5   Continue this abdominal breathing (holding your stomach
    out when you breathe in and your stomach in when you
    breathe out), with the pauses between breathing in and
    out and between breathing out and in, but direct the
    expelled air in turn to:

a   your heels   n   the nape of your neck
b   your left leg   o   the top of your back*
c   your right leg   p   the centre of your back*
d   your left thigh   q   your lower back*
e   your right thigh   r   your left shoulder
f   your left buttock*   s   your right shoulder
g   your right buttock*   t   your left arm
h   your genitals   u   your right arm
i   your abdomen   v   your left forearm
j   your chest   w   your right forearm
k   your neck   x   your left hand
l   your face   y   your right hand
m   the top of your head

And every time you do this, make sure you relax the part
of your body to which you are directing your breath,
whether in reality or just in your imagination.

Useful tip

If you want it to work really well, after you have learned
this technique properly you should practise it once a day or
every other day, preferably in the morning.

* In your imagination

22 The Pitch-dark Technique

When to use: for tiredness, general toning up, prevention of stress.

This technique, developed by J.-J. Dexter, puts you into a brief, extremely relaxing, hypnotic sleep. It is a good idea to supplement it with some gentle relaxing music played at low volume, which will also be useful in limiting the length of your sleep to the amount of time you have at your disposal.

Step-by-step guide

1 Make sure you will not be disturbed during this session and find a place away from any noise. The room should be in darkness, except for the light of a single candle.
2 Sit yourself comfortably in an armchair, with the lighted candle in front of you. Place your feet flat on the floor, a little apart with the toes turned in. Your arms should be resting on the arms of the chair, as should your hands, unless you prefer to have them hanging over the edge. Make sure your back is properly supported, and lean your head back against the chair so that it is resting in

its normal position, neither too far back nor falling forward.

3 Relax all the muscles in your body, and empty your mind of every thought except this: 'I am going to rest and I am going to feel good, really good.'

4 Keep on repeating this until you have absolutely convinced yourself: 'I am going to rest and I am going to feel good, really good.'

5 Fix your eyes on the candle flame and think only of this flame.

6 Let yourself become completely absorbed by this point of light, and say to yourself: 'The longer I look at this flame, the heavier my body is growing . . . it is growing heavier and heavier . . .'

7 When this feeling of heaviness has spread through your entire body, close your eyes, but keep the image of the candle flame in your mind (it will stay on the screen in your brain for several moments), but let it grow blurred and fade away by itself, and as it does so, say to yourself: 'All the time that the darkness is slowly engulfing this flame, my body is growing heavier and heavier . . . heavier and heavier all the time.'

8 When your mental image of the flame has faded away, keeping your eyes closed, say to yourself: 'All that remains for me is this darkness, this dark chasm absorbing all my thoughts, a darkness that makes my head heavy, heavier and heavier . . . I feel tired, very tired . . . Even if I wanted to, I couldn't move now . . . I feel sleepy, so sleepy . . . I shan't resist it . . . I shall just let myself go . . . All around me and inside me everything is dark, everything is heavy . . . I am falling asleep . . . I can't resist sleep any longer . . . Sleep is entering into every pore . . . sleep is coming and I can't resist it any more . . . I am asleep . . . The music is rocking me, I am asleep . . . I am sleeping more and more deeply . . . Nothing exists but this sleep . . . this pleasant sleep . . . this gentle sleep . . . this sleep as gentle as the music I

hear . . . a very deep sleep . . . I feel good, very good . . .
My head and all my body are resting . . . I am asleep . . .
The music is my only link with the world . . . I am
asleep . . . I am asleep . . . Soon, the music will stop and
then I shall wake up . . . But now I am sleeping, I am
still sleeping . . . Sleeping is good . . . sleeping is restful
. . . I am sleeping . . . sleeping . . .'

9   When the music stops, say to yourself: 'The music has
stopped. My head is feeling lighter, lighter and lighter,
I can open my eyes . . . I am awake!'

Useful tips

Usually after five or six attempts, you will be able to
achieve the desired effect from this technique. Later on,
you will not always have to resort to music but will find
that you can vary the length of the sleep at will, notably by
setting a time limit on it (five minutes, quarter of an hour,
and so on). Similarly, you will only need the other conditions (solitude, quiet, the candle and armchair) in the
early sessions: after several weeks' training with a session a
day, it will usually become possible to practise this method
anywhere, whether you are on your own or not, in full
daylight, without needing to fix on a luminous point, and
sitting on a hard chair or even a bench.

You can also replace the music with a metronome if you
prefer. It should be regulated to a very slow beat, with an
interval of two or three seconds between each movement.
You must:

● breathe in deeply at the first swing of the pendulum
(between the tick and the tock);
● breathe out deeply during the second swing . . . and
continue to synchronise the rhythm of your breathing
with the rhythm of the pendulum, and after you have
achieved total darkness in your mind, say to yourself:
'The more I breath, the more I am asleep . . .'

23 The Heaviness Technique

When to use: for insomnia.

This method was once again developed by the hypnotist J.-J. Dexter, and is intended to produce a hypnotic sleep that will develop into a normal one.

Step-by-step guide

1 Lie on your back in a comfortable position, with your feet, legs, arms and hands resting naturally, totally supported by the bed.
2 Close your eyes and concentrate your thoughts on the idea of relaxing, and say to yourself: 'I am relaxing . . . my whole body is relaxing . . .'
3 When you have relaxed all your muscles, turn your mind to your body: concentrate first on your toes, then the soles of your feet, your heels, your shins, your knees and thighs, and continue to progress up your body like this until you reach the top of your head.
4 Say to yourself in your mind: 'I have thought of every part of my body . . . My body is there, stretched out on

the bed, and each part of my body corresponds to a weight, a very heavy weight . . . getting heavier and heavier . . . The feeling of heaviness is spreading all over my head . . . Like a compact, solid cloud, the weight is pressing down on my brain and my brain is growing heavy, heavier and heavier . . . The heaviness is still in my head, but now it is spreading . . . I can feel the weight in my neck . . . in my shoulders . . . in my chest . . . in my stomach . . . in my belly . . . in my thighs . . . in my knees . . . in my shins . . . in my feet . . .'

5 Imagine your body stretched on the bed, inseparable from it, as though it were nailed to it, completely crushed by the invisible weight dominating your body from head to toe.

6 Say to yourself: 'My body is surrounded in darkness and this dark is slowly engulfing me . . . I feel heavy, heavy . . . I am imprisoned by a heaviness I cannot explain . . . It's impossible to move . . . I can't resist the darkness engulfing my feet . . . my shins . . . my knees . . . my thighs . . . My head is heavy . . . it's so heavy that I can no longer watch the darkness which has now completely swallowed up my legs and is still rising . . . I know that I am going to go to sleep . . . My head and my whole body are heavy, too heavy . . . And the darkness is advancing . . . Gradually, the darkness is coming up to my neck . . . My body has been absorbed by the dark right up to my neck . . . My head will be swallowed up by the dark and I'm going to let it happen . . . The dark will bring me sleep, I shall let it happen . . . My chin has disappeared in the darkness . . . the darkness now covers my lips . . . my nose . . . my cheeks . . . my ears . . . It has reached my forehead . . . it's not stopping . . . it's still coming . . . it has reached the top of my head . . . It's total darkness. I am completely absorbed by the dark . . . I am overcome with sleep . . . I am sleeping, sleeping . . . sleeping . . .'

Useful tips

The power of your imagination and the intensity of your resolve to be 'completely absorbed' by the imaginary sensation of heaviness and darkness have an important role to play. Since these factors vary from one individual to another, it is impossible to say for certain how long, on average, this exercise will last. One can say however that:

- if the experiment is successful, it will, in its first stage, produce a hypnotic sleep (varying from a few minutes to an hour or more), from which will follow, in the second stage, a natural calm and regular sleep, free of nightmares;
- success will depend on the nature of the insomnia: whether it is chronic or not (if not, then, it goes without saying, there will be fewer difficulties);
- in the same way, some of you will be able to manage less than five minutes' hypnotic sleep (in the first stage), but if there are certain 'blocks', the process of inducement will be considerably slowed down in subjects who do not readily respond to self-hypnosis;
- as a general rule, at the end of a certain time (a period which can vary between one and four weeks), normal sleep, which had been disrupted by insomnia, will feature regularly in your life again, and you will reach a stage where you will no longer need to resort to self-hypnosis as a prelude.

24 The Fixation Technique

When to use: for insomnia.

This is another method by J.-J. Dexter. This one relies on one of the standard procedures used in inducing hypnosis: prolonged fixation on a precise point, which can be either luminous or not.

Step-by-step guide

1 Lie on your back in a place where you find it easiest to relax and where you can feel in a perfect state of repose.
2 Empty your mind of every thought except: 'I want to sleep and I am going to sleep'.
3 Choose some point or other on the ceiling just above your head, and fix your eyes on this point (if the room is not lit, you can use some imaginary point to fix on).
4 Think only of this (imaginary or real) point and say to yourself: 'I am thinking only of this point, all my attention is concentrated on this one point, right there, just above me, which is going to absorb my complete attention, I won't be able to take my eyes away from it . . . My eyelids are growing heavy . . . they are

becoming heavier and heavier . . . My eyes are beginning to tire, but I am still fixing on the point . . . the point which has become my whole world . . . My eyelids are becoming extremely heavy . . . My eyes are becoming extremely tired . . . My eyelids are so heavy and my eyes are so tired that I can't go on any longer . . . I am closing my eyes . . . Now that my eyes are shut I feel good, I feel relaxed . . . But that point on the ceiling is still there in my mind, I have the feeling I can still "see" it . . . My thoughts would like to wander, but I am still thinking of the point, solely of the point . . . Everything is dark around the point, which is now so tiny that I can hardly see it, but I am forcing myself to see it and I can't see anything but that . . . My brain is tired . . . My head is beginning to feel overwhelmingly heavy . . . I can't fix on the point any more . . . I am letting myself go, I am letting the darkness invade the screen of my brain completely . . . Now there's nothing but blackness . . . Everything is black . . . I feel weary . . . Thinking is impossible, the darkness dominates everything . . . I've reached a stage where I'm no longer in control, the darkness has become an abyss, a pleasant, gentle abyss, the dark has engulfed everything around me and within me, the darkness is sleep, a heavy, deep sleep . . . I feel good . . . I am letting go . . . I'm letting myself be carried off into the darkness . . . I am going down, down to the bottom of the abyss . . . the darkness is rocking me . . . I am sleeping . . . I am asleep . . . asleep . . .'

Useful tips

This technique is especially recommended if you have a mild sleep problem, and will put you into a hypnotic sleep that will develop into a natural one; but it also has the other characteristics of Technique no. 23, as regards the length of time the whole experience will take and so on (see Useful tips, p. 95).

25 The Flame and Escalator Technique

When to use: for all the problems listed on pp. 25–6.

As we have already seen in Technique no. 7, prolonged contemplation of a candle flame can have a hypnotic effect, so it is no surprise that leading specialists in medical hypnosis (among them Le Cron) have developed combined techniques that make use of this.

Step-by-step guide

1 Find a room where you can be on your own and, if possible, away from any kind of noise. It should be lit only by the flame of a candle.
2 Settle yourself comfortably in an armchair, with the candle in front of you, and concentrate your entire attention on this source of light.
3 Say to yourself: 'I am looking at the flame, all I am thinking about is the flame . . . As time passes, my eyelids are growing heavy, heavier and heavier . . . Soon my eyelids will be so heavy that they will close all by themselves, and I won't be able to stop them . . .

My eyelids are growing heavier and heavier . . . My eyes are going to shut and I shall be in a state of self-hypnosis . . .'

4 When your eyes have closed, say to yourself: 'I am relaxing the muscles in my arms . . . in my legs . . . in my whole body . . . My tension is going and I am becoming less and less tense . . .'

5 As soon as your feeling of tension begins to disappear from your whole body, imagine a moving staircase (it can be going up or down, whichever you like, but if you experience any feelings of anxiety on an escalator that is going down, but don't have any feeling of fear when it is going up, then you must imagine it going up) and step on to it, saying to yourself: 'The higher (lower) this escalator takes me, the more relaxed I feel . . . more and more relaxed . . . The higher (lower) the escalator goes, the more relaxed I feel . . .'

6 Once you have achieved this feeling of relaxation, imagine yourself in a particularly pleasant place (a wood, or by the sea, for example) and move on to the self-hypnotic suggestion stage, which first of all concentrates on a feeling of general well-being, of total comfort and complete serenity, then on your resolve to do your best to:

- fight sickness or pain;
- avoid stress;
- give up smoking, alcohol, etc.;
- calm your nerves;
- conquer your aggression;
- increase your productivity . . . and so on.

In each case repeat the appropriate formula to fulfil the aim of the session, for example:

- 'I shall follow my doctor's prescriptions to the letter.'
- 'I shall ignore the pain I feel in such and such a part of my body.'

- 'I shall hold on to the relaxed feeling I am experiencing at the moment, whatever happens.'
- 'I have no interest in smoking (alcohol, drugs, sweets, etc.).'
- 'I shall always have the greatest confidence in my abilities.'
- 'Nothing is going to make me angry.'
- 'Nothing's going to stop me from giving my best.' And so on.

Useful tips

Watching the flame is often used in religious and esoteric circles to bring on a sort of trance state as a preliminary to meditation (the term 'hypnotic state' is carefully avoided). In the case of the technique which has just been described, a fixation such as this on a luminous point will successfully achieve authentic self-hypnosis, but you will need to deepen it if you want to be able to programme a suggestion to keep a resolution you have made, in ideal conditions.

26 The Contrasting Colours Technique

When to use: for all the problems listed on pp. 25–6.

An optical phenomenon caused by gazing continuously at contrasting colours forms the basis of this technique. To practise it you will need a special piece of equipment: a piece of grey cardboard, roughly the same size and shape as a postcard, but a little larger, on which are two rectangles, the left one yellow and the right one blue, separated by a small space.

Step-by-step guide

1 Settle down in your most comfortable armchair, or stretch out on a bed, divan or sofa.
2 Hold the card with the contrasting colours in your right hand (or if you are left-handed, in your left hand) and bring it up level with your face, holding your arm so that the yellow rectangle is directly opposite your left eye.
3 Fix your gaze continuously on both rectangles, more especially on the space between them.

4 When the phenomenon of colour contrast occurs (this will take the form both of visual modification and a change in your state of awareness: you will have the impression of seeing blue on the left and yellow on the right, or in some cases the intensity of the colours will seem to change, the image will waver, and so on), say to yourself: 'My vision is disturbed, this marks the beginning of self-hypnosis and means that my state of consciousness is changing . . . My eyes are tired . . . My eyelids are beginning to feel heavy . . . heavier and heavier . . . Soon, my eyelids will droop, and I won't be able to stop them . . . It's impossible to keep my eyes open . . . My eyes are closing . . . Now my right arm (left arm for left-handed) is becoming heavy, very heavy, heavier and heavier . . . So heavy that it's impossible for me to keep holding it up . . . I cannot help it, my arm is sinking . . . It's an enormous effort to keep gripping the card . . . I can't hold the card any longer, I am letting it fall . . . Now it's the turn of my other arm to become heavy, so heavy, heavier and heavier . . . Both my arms are heavy, terribly heavy, I can't move them any more . . . The heavier my arms feel, the deeper my self-hypnosis. And now the heaviness has moved to my shoulders as well . . . and my neck . . . my head . . . Now the feeling of heaviness is travelling down my body . . . it has reached my chest . . . my stomach . . . my belly . . . The more this feeling of heaviness progresses, the deeper and deeper becomes my self-hypnosis . . . My thighs are heavy, heavier and heavier . . . My feet are heavy, heavier and heavier . . . My whole body is heavy, it could not be heavier . . . I am in a deep state of self-hypnosis . . . I am in a deep state of self-hypnosis . . . I am in a deep state of self-hypnosis . . .'

5 Repeat, three or four times: 'The self-hypnotic state I am in enables me to influence my subconscious.'

6 Say to yourself: 'Now I can take advantage of my

102

self-hypnosis . . . Now I can be constructive . . .'
and direct the suggestion towards your objective, as
indicated in the description of the sixth step of Technique no. 25 on pp. 99–100.

Useful tips

This technique, developed by the author, also has a version for use when hypnotising another person. However,
whether it is used with someone else or for self-hypnosis,
this phenomenon of colour contrast is a great help in
hastening the onset of hypnosis.

27 The Combined Technique

When to use: for all the problems listed on pp. 25–6.

This technique must be learned under the supervision of a qualified hypnotherapist.

Step-by-step instruction guide

1   The hypnotherapist will say something along these lines: 'If I tell you that you will succeed in hypnotising yourself, in other words that you will undergo self-hypnosis, it is because it really is possible. My job is to help you benefit from a training that will be very satisfying for you. But it is vital that you follow my instructions to the letter.

'First of all, let me make it clear that familiarisation with the technique I am going to teach you requires no special effort on your part. All you have to do is focus your attention, even if only for a fraction of a second. When you have done that, I shall step in to help you enter into a particular state that will be extremely beneficial to you.

'You must also realise that, in order to reach your self-hypnotic state I shall, if need be, resort to the most appropriate methods and that these methods have all been properly tested and are completely harmless . . .

'Otherwise, all I need tell you is this: in the course of the session, at a given moment, you will experience real pleasure in swallowing. This sensation will be the sign that the experiment has been successful, and you will be able to conclude from it that you are in a state of deep self-hypnosis . . .'

2   The patient is then asked to settle into a comfortable position, either in an armchair or lying on his or her back (on a divan or sofa), and to relax completely.

3   Once the hypnotherapist is satisfied that the patient is sufficiently relaxed, he will continue:

'Close your eyes . . . Concentrate all your attention on your saliva . . . Very soon, you will feel an urge to swallow . . . The moment you swallow you will be in a self-hypnotic state . . . Continue focusing all your attention on your saliva. In a short while you are bound to want to swallow . . . You have an urge to swallow . . . You can't resist it, you have an urge to swallow . . . I am going to count to fifteen . . . When I say "fifteen", your need to swallow will be so strong that you will automatically swallow a few seconds later . . . You may well feel you have to swallow long before I reach "fifteen" . . . Whenever it happens, that swallowing will be a sign that your self-hypnosis is real . . . Soon, you are going to feel your mouth watering, you will be swallowing . . . That will prove you are near your goal . . . Your salivation, your swallowing will prove that you have achieved self-hypnosis, the beginning of your new way of life . . . As soon as you begin to salivate, to swallow, everything about you will change . . . nothing will be able to irritate you . . . every trace of tiredness will disappear, every trace of stress . . . You will be in self-hypnosis . . .

And every time your mouth waters, every time you swallow, your self-hypnotic state will become deeper and more pleasant . . .'

4 Slowly the hypnotherapist will count to fifteen and, between each number, will repeat the suggestion: 'Your urge to swallow is growing stronger and stronger . . . You are getting closer and closer to self-hypnosis . . .'

5 When the counting has finished, if the patient has swallowed with obvious pleasure, he or she is praised; if not, no comment is made.

6 Whether or not the patient has swallowed, the hypnotherapist follows up with another suggestion:

'Imagine that your body is squashy like rubber . . . Say to yourself: "My body is squashy like rubber" . . . Keeping your eyes closed, focus all your attention on the mental picture of a squashy rubber man . . . and say to yourself: "I am like this rubber man, all squashy . . ." You feel all squashy . . . If you do, it's because your self-hypnosis is increasing . . . Each exercise will deepen your self-hypnosis . . .

'You are in self-hypnosis, you are feeling good, very good . . . But I can tell you are not yet completely free of extraneous thoughts, thoughts that disturb your relaxed state. So now we are going to progress even further, and more methodically . . . When we have gone that far, you will be able to change yourself . . . You are no longer going to be a victim, full of anxieties,[1] you are going to change completely, have a new identity which will be built up day by day in your mind . . .

'I've got a pleasant surprise for you . . . In a few moments I shall put my hand on your forehead and this will make all your negative, unpleasant, agonising

[1] At this point, the hypnotherapist will mention the point of the treatment (illness, smoking addiction, nervousness and so on).

thoughts disappear for a long time; all those unrelent-
ing, tormenting thoughts that wear you out . . . And
that's not all . . . When I put my hand on your
forehead, you will have a wonderful surprise: you will
be able to enter into the world of your subconscious . . .
With such insight you will be able to identify the deep
cause of your problems and discover how they can be
resolved . . .'

7　The hypnotherapist places his hand on the patient's
forehead and says:

'Because I have put my hand on your forehead, your
mind is now closed to negative, harmful thoughts
for a long time to come. Notice how well you feel,
how completely relaxed and serene . . . Yes, you are
experiencing true inner peace . . . Your sense of great
peace is creating ideal conditions for your mind to
explore the new possibilities that are being revealed to
you . . . You are in a hypnotic state and it is impossible
for you to do other than follow my instructions . . .'

8　At this stage, appropriate advice is given, according to
the patient's needs (fighting against illness, pain, stress
and so on) and also according to such factors as his or
her personality, lifestyle and so on.

9　The hypnotherapist continues:

'The extraordinary state of relaxation that you are
experiencing at this moment allows you not only to be
perfectly aware of what you should do to overcome
your problems, but also totally to remove all the social
and other constraints that prevent you from realising
your ambitions . . . You feel capable of surmounting
every obstacle in your way . . .'

10　The hypnotherapist goes on to suggest that the patient
should raise an arm:

'Soon your right arm (left arm for the left-handed)
will feel light, lighter and lighter . . . While I am talking
to you, your arm will feel lighter and lighter . . . As the
moments tick by, your arm will become lighter and

lighter . . . as light as a feather . . . as light as air . . . Imagine balloons attached to your wrist . . .'

11 Gently the doctor touches the patient's right wrist (or if the patient is left-handed, the left wrist) and continues:

'Yes, blue balloons, pink balloons, red balloons, yellow balloons and green balloons are attached to your wrist . . . A host of beautiful balloons . . . And, soon, they are going to take off . . . Soon these balloons attached to your wrist are going to draw your right (left) arm up into the air . . . Pulled by these balloons, your right (left) hand, then your right (left) arm will rise, inexorably . . . Your arm will be as light as the balloons, as light as the air that fills them . . . There they go, the balloons have taken off . . . Blue, red, green, yellow, the balloons are pulling your right (left) arm up into the air. Irresistibly drawn up by the balloons, your arm is going to rise with them . . . The balloons are rising, rising . . . still rising . . . rising even higher . . . The balloons are rising . . . higher . . . still higher . . . your right (left) arm is light . . . light . . . light . . . Your arm is as weightless as these balloons . . . as weightless as air . . . It's lifting with the balloons . . . lift . . . lift . . . notice how extraordinarily light your arm is . . . The balloons are flying . . . flying . . . They are taking your arm with them . . . they are taking you with them . . . You even feel that you are floating above your body . . . You feel free . . . light . . . happy . . .'

12 If necessary, the hypnotherapist will repeat the suggestion of the arm being pulled upwards by balloons, and in that case, might even take hold of the patient's arm to help him or her raise it. Then he says:

'Now, your right (left) arm is going to bend . . . Very gently, your arm is going to bend . . . Your arm will come down . . . come down, until your hand can touch your forehead . . . And when your hand touches your forehead, you are going to slide into a self-hypnotic state that is a hundred times deeper than the one you are in now . . . Your arm is coming down . . . coming down . . . Your hand is getting near your forehead . . . Your hand is getting nearer and nearer your forehead . . . In a moment your hand will touch your forehead . . .'

13 As soon as the patient's hand touches his or her forehead, the hypnotist quickly praises the patient for following the suggestion correctly, then adds:

'. . . Now that your right (left) hand is resting on your forehead, your self-hypnotic state is a hundred times deeper than it was a few moments ago . . . But you can go even deeper . . . I am now going to take your arm, very gently, and I am going to place it on the divan (arm of the chair) . . . And as soon as your arm is on the divan (arm of the chair) your self-hypnotic state will be even deeper than it is now . . .'

14 The hypnotherapist then softly takes the patient's right (left) arm to place it on the divan (arm of the chair), explaining as he does so:

'By putting your arm on the divan (arm of the chair), I am making your self-hypnotic state deeper, which will allow you to feel even more relaxed, even more resolved to overcome the problem that made you decide to practise self-hypnosis . . . What's more, now that your arm is lying by your body on the divan (arm of the chair), you are enjoying a hypnotic state deep enough for us to be able to communicate successfully with your subconscious . . . Yes, from now on all you will have to do to put yourself into a state of self-hypnosis is repeat to yourself in your mind five times: "My right (left) arm is as light as air" . . . Your right (left) arm is as light as air . . . Your right (left) arm is as light as air . . . Go on, learn to put yourself into self-hypnosis . . . Repeat in your head five times: "My right (left) arm is as light as air . . ." '

15 After giving the patient time to carry out his instruction, he continues:

'With your right (left) arm as light as air, you are in self-hypnosis and free from the burden of your tensions . . . The lighter your right (left) arm, the more relaxed you are . . . And now you are going to be able to experience for yourself the direct link that has been established between you and your subconscious . . . It's simple: all you have to do is think, "My right (left) arm is as light as air", and immediately your subconscious will make your arm as light as air . . . You can prove it, it works . . . You can put yourself into a self-hypnotic state without the slightest difficulty . . . And you can fight the illness, the pain, the stress and all the problems encountered in everyday life . . . I myself am going to activate your subconscious, so that it can fly to your aid whenever you need it . . . By saying your surname and first name [he does so] . . . I am addressing your subconscious and ensuring that it will come to your aid at any time, allowing you to relax, to change, to metamorphose, to become a new person, healthy, balanced, confident, brave, determined [here, the proposals should be geared to the needs of the individual] . . . I promise you that, because you have learned how to practise self-hypnosis, you will actually be able to trigger an automatic conditioned reflex under any circumstances, even the most stressful . . . You will say this sentence in your head five times: "My right (left) arm is as light as air", you will salivate three times and without fail you will be in a self-hypnotic state.'

16 It is advisable to pause for a minute or two, before suggesting going down (or up, if the patient prefers) a staircase. The hypnotherapist says:

'Imagine you are at the top (bottom) of a staircase with fifty steps . . . You are going to go down (up) this staircase, and with each step you will be deepening your self-hypnosis even further . . . Off you go, begin walking down (up) . . . Take the first step down (up), and you will find yourself on level number one, and you can say to yourself, "I am taking the first step down (up), I am at my number-one level and therefore I am deepening my self-hypnosis" . . . Now for the second step . . . say to yourself, "I am taking the second step down (up), I am deepening my self-hypnosis even more . . ." '

Tirelessly, the hypnotherapist continues to guide the patient in this way until he or she has reached the bottom (top) of the stairs, the level at which suggestion brings with it the realisation of the most total kind of relaxation, and the achievement of the deepest possible self-hypnosis.

17 When the mental descent (ascent) of the staircase has been completed, the time is right to programme a phase that is one of the major stages found in many hypnotising procedures. This is *post-hypnotic suggestion*. The hypnotherapist will go on:

'Now that you are totally relaxed, now that you are in the deepest possible self-hypnotic state, I can give you the keyword . . . This keyword will enable you to go into a self-hypnotic state, or if you are already in one, to go into an even deeper one . . . Yes, in any situation, all you will have to do is repeat in your head, three times, the keyword I am about to tell you and you will immediately slide into self-hypnosis or, if you are already in a self-hypnotic state, through this keyword you will be able to reach an even deeper state of self-hypnosis . . . Now, here it is: your keyword or, if you prefer, your code word, is "Fakir"[1] . . . To deepen your self-hypnosis, I say, "Fakir" . . . "Fakir" . . . "Fakir" . . . and you repeat in your head, "Fakir" . . . "Fakir" . . . "Fakir".'

18 After waiting in silence for a few minutes, the hypno-

---

[1] This is only an example. The hypnotherapist will select a keyword that seems most appropriate for a particular patient.

therapist proceeds to awaken the patient:

'And now it's time to come back . . . As I say "one", the self-hypnosis will wear off . . . As I say "two", you will wake up . . . As I say "three", you are awake, feeling fresh and full of energy.'

Useful tips

This technique is called 'combined self-hypnosis' because it uses suggestions that are made up of three different aspects (salivation and swallowing, imagining the weightlessness of the arms, and use of the keyword or code). The technique was developed by the author and has the advantage of making self-hypnosis readily accessible – even for those who previously have always failed to enter into a self-hypnotic state.

28 The Magnetism Technique

When to use: for all the problems listed on pp. 25–6.

This technique, like the previous one, should only be attempted with the guidance of a qualified hypnotherapist.

Step-by-step instruction guide

1 The hypnotherapist asks the patient to sit comfortably, facing him, and says:
    'I am sure you already know what human magnetism is. Well, I am lucky enough to possess a particularly powerful magnetic fluid. You will be able to see this for yourself . . . So hold my fingers in your hands. I shall then be able to transmit a part of my magnetic fluid to you, a part of the energy that will revitalise you. So that you can be revitalised, I am going to transmit a part of my magnetic fluid, and for a good minute I shall say nothing, but simply concentrate on transmitting this revitalising energy . . .'
2 After about a minute's silence, the hypnotist continues:
    'Now that you are fresh and full of energy, we are

going to move on to an exercise . . . You are going to squeeze my fingers hard . . . Go on, squeeze them, harder and harder . . . Harder still . . . You can't let go of my fingers any more . . . the more you try to let them go, the less you will be able to . . . You are squeezing my fingers, it's impossible for you not to squeeze my fingers, and while you are squeezing my fingers you are becoming stronger and stronger, you can squeeze them harder and harder . . .'

3   If this experiment is inconclusive, the hypnotist will persist until the patient fully responds to the suggestion, at which stage he will continue:

'Now I am going to withdraw my hand, slowly . . . And since you can't let go of my hand, your hands will be forced to follow the movement of mine . . .'

4   Gently, the hypnotherapist withdraws his hand, saying:

'Your hands are firmly attached to mine . . . I am withdrawing my hand, it is impossible for you to let go, your hands are following the movement of my hand . . . And now, I am going to count backwards, from "three" to "one" . . . When I say "one", not only will you be able to release my hand, but you will be in a special state, open to self-hypnotic suggestion . . . Yes, when I say "one", you will be in a state that will enable you to learn how to trigger your self-hypnosis instantly, by using a code word . . . I am saying "three" . . . You are going to learn through a code word how to enter a self-hypnotic state . . . I am saying "two" . . . In a few moments, your hands will release mine and you will be ready to learn the code word for your self-hypnosis . . . I am saying "one" . . . Your hands are releasing mine . . . You are experiencing a feeling of relaxation . . . Enjoy it, relax even more, close your eyes, so that you can relax further . . . And now that you are quite relaxed, I am going to teach you your code word . . . And when I say this code word three times, you will slide into a self-hypnotic state . . . Yes, all it needs is for me to say this code word three times and you will be self-hypnotised ... Whether you keep your eyes closed or open them, you will experience a delicious sensation of inner peace ... This delicious sensation of inner peace will enable you to make contact with your subconscious ...'

5   Once the patient's attitude shows that he or she is receptive (in other words, at the stage where there is no need to repeat the suggestions), the hypnotist will continue:

'Here it is, your code word that will enable you to enter a self-hypnotic state. It is made up of a vowel, "A", and three consonants, "H", "S" and "K". So your code word is "AHSK" ... I am shortly going to say this code word "AHSK" three times in a row and then you will be in self-hypnosis ... That means that, from that moment, whether you are sitting in front of me or are thousands of miles from my office, at the mention of the word "AHSK" you will automatically enter into self-hypnosis ... Yes from that moment, when I say "AHSK" in your presence, or when I say it to you over the telephone, you will only have to hear it three times to find yourself immediately in the pleasant state you are in at the moment ... And what's more, you will be totally obliged to do everything I ask you to do in your interest, to help you overcome this illness or whatever problem you have ... Now that we've got all that quite clear, in order for the words I have just said to be planted more firmly in your subconscious, I am going to stay silent for a few moments.'

6   After a brief pause, he continues:

'When I say "AHSK" three times, one after the other, you will slide into self-hypnosis ... the code word "AHSK" will trigger your self-hypnosis automatically and instantaneously ... Every time you hear me say "AHSK" three times in a row, you will be in a state to absorb, into your innermost being, everything

I say to you for your own good.'

7   He moves on to the waking-up stage, using a formula similar to the one used in Technique no. 27:

'And now it's time to come back. As I say "one" the self-hypnosis fades away . . . As I say "two" you are waking up . . . As I say "three" you are awake, fresh and full of energy.'

8   A test is then carried out: the hypnotist pronounces the keyword three times in a row . . .

9   If the test is conclusive, he will use the patient's hypnotic state to confer on him or her the power to enter into a self-hypnotic state independently:

'Everything I say to you will remain engraved in your memory. From this moment on, at any time, wherever you are, all you will have to do is say the code word "AHSK" three times in a row, either out loud or in your head, simply by thinking it, and you will instantly be in self-hypnosis, in the pleasant, totally relaxed state you are in now . . .'

He repeats this suggestion twice more.

10   The patient wakes up (using the formula in step no. 7) and, shortly afterwards, is invited to put him- or herself into a state of self-hypnosis, using the keyword either out loud or in the mind.

11   If the patient succeeds in putting him- or herself into self-hypnosis, the hypnotist will continue as follows:

'Now we are going to try an experiment that will help you familiarise yourself with remote-controlled hypnosis or, if you prefer, with the phenomenon of telepathy . . . Right, I am going to go into the next room and I shall do something there that will make something happen in you . . . You may experience a feeling of heaviness, or numbness, or a need to sleep, or you may want to salivate, or swallow . . . Or else you may, quite simply, experience a very pleasant feeling of well-being . . . For this to happen I shall, perhaps, use the code word, but that's not certain . . .

In any event, there are two possibilities: either you will feel something, or you will feel nothing . . . For the moment, all you have to do is wait, calmly, serenely . . . One thing is certain: it's an odd fact that when I am next door and concentrating on you, the more you attempt to resist me, the more you will be driven to obey me . . .'

12 The hypnotherapist then goes into the next room and, as he promised, mentally directs instructions to the patient for about two minutes.

13 When he returns, he studies the patient, then questions him or her about the sensations that he or she experienced. (This type of verification is obviously useful, as it provides indications of the reactions that the patient could have in the course of the forthcoming hypnotherapy.)

14 The next day, it is recommended that hypnotist and patient go on to consolidate the suggestions given. For that the patient must telephone the hypnotist, who will say to him or her:

'Sit comfortably . . . Hold the telephone in one hand and keep the other one free. Practise abdominal breathing . . . with your stomach out when you breathe in and your stomach in when you breathe out . . . Carry on like this and notice how your stomach rises . . . and how it falls . . . In a moment I shall say that code word of yours, three times in a row . . . As soon as I do this, your eyes will close and you will slide into self-hypnosis . . . You will feel an inner peace . . . You will experience a marvellous feeling of relaxation and you will be able to make direct contact with your subconscious . . . In a flash, you will find yourself in the pleasant state you were in yesterday during our session. As soon as I use the code word, you will have absolutely no choice but to return to a self-hypnotic state. Right, in a moment I am going to say the code word . . . I am saying the code word . . . "AHSK" . . .

"AHSK" . . . "AHSK" . . . Go on breathing with your stomach out when you breathe in and your stomach in when you breathe out . . . With each breath you take, your self-hypnosis is deepening . . . Your self-hypnosis is strengthening more and more . . . Your subconscious is registering everything I say perfectly . . . You are going to be cured . . . You will be cured . . .'

Useful tips

This particularly powerful technique can be used to fight an illness, for detoxification or as an aid to learning. The hypnotherapist can also take measures to reinforce the self-hypnosis he has activated. To do this, the patient is asked to bring in a book of his choice (healthy reading, of course) and the hypnotherapist writes 'AHSK' in big letters on a number of pieces of paper, then says to the patient:

'I am putting these bits of paper with the code word "AHSK" written on them between certain pages of your book. When you read this book, whether you are at home or anywhere else, every time you come across the word "AHSK" in my writing you will enter into a self-hypnotic state automatically and without your eyes closing . . . Every time you read the code word "AHSK" in my writing, you will enter into self-hypnosis and will revive your resolve to fight the illness (pain, stress and so on), using the instructions I have given you (that I will give you) . . .'

If the aim is to help the patient pass an exam or win a contest, the formula to use is as follows:

'When you read the code word "AHSK", you will automatically enter into self-hypnosis and your eyes will remain open . . . You are going to write the code word "AHSK" at the top of every page of the textbooks that you are using for your exam or contest . . . Reading the code word will enable you to go into self-hypnosis and so take in more easily the information printed on the page in question . . . Your eyes will remain open and, because you are in self-hypnosis, you will have no trouble remembering all that you have to learn to pass your exam (win the contest) . . . Reading the code word "AHSK" will activate your memory, and enable you to work more easily . . . it will be like child's play . . . And to end your self-hypnotic state, all you will have to do is close your eyes and say to yourself, five times, in your head: "I am going to come out of self-hypnosis . . ." '

29 The Sophrological Karate Technique

When to use: for all the problems listed on pp. 25–6.

This technique was perfected by the author, and incorporates his method of sophrological karate. This is a system that combines many elements: it is a way of restoring the body's energy balance; a therapeutic sport; an original combination of physical and psychological exercises; a way of achieving muscular relaxation using mental imagery; a form of psychotherapy which draws on the martial arts (in particular, karate); it is a philosophy, a discipline for self-control, a method of reinforcing the personality and a sense of responsibility; it is a factor in developing an individual's ability to 'become an integral part of the Universe', a link between Eastern and Western psychologies . . . but it is also a digest of techniques for self-defence, a breathing technique, a massage technique for the psychic points used in self-acupuncture, and a physical method of eliminating muscular tension.

Step-by-step guide

1 Lie on your back and say to yourself: 'I am lying down and I feel calm', as many times as you need – that is, until you genuinely feel this.

2 Say to yourself (and, if necessary, repeat it): 'I am relaxing all the muscles in my body' and banish every thought from your mind except this all-over muscular relaxation.

3 Say to yourself, twice: 'I am relaxing the muscles in my hands' . . . and do it.

4 Say to yourself, twice: 'I am relaxing the muscles in my forearms' . . . and do it.

5 Say to yourself, twice: 'I am relaxing the muscles in my arms' . . . and do it.

6 Say to yourself, twice: 'I am relaxing the muscles in my shoulders' . . . and do it.

7 Say to yourself, twice: 'I am relaxing the muscles in my feet' . . . and do it.

8 Say to yourself, twice: 'I am relaxing the muscles in my calves' . . . and do it.

9 Say to yourself, twice: 'I am relaxing the muscles in my thighs' . . . and do it.

10 Repeat four or five times to yourself: 'My arms are heavy' . . . and imagine your arms turned into sacks that are gradually filling up with lead.

11 Repeat four or five times to yourself: 'My legs are heavy' . . . and imagine, again, that your legs have been turned into sacks that are gradually filling up with lead.

12 Say to yourself, twice: 'I am relaxing the muscles in my forehead' . . . and do it.

13 Say to yourself, twice: 'I am relaxing the muscles in the back of my head' . . . and do it.

14 Say to yourself, twice: 'I am relaxing the muscles in my mouth' . . . and do it.

15 Say to yourself, twice: 'I am relaxing the muscles in my nose' . . . and do it.

16 Say to yourself, twice: 'I am relaxing my eye muscles' ... and do it.

17 Say to yourself, twice: 'I am relaxing my ear muscles' ... and do it.

18 Say to yourself, twice: 'I am relaxing the muscles in my neck' ... and do it.

19 Say to yourself, twice: 'I am relaxing the muscles in my chest' ... and do it.

20 Say to yourself, twice: 'I am relaxing the muscles in my abdomen' ... and do it.

21 Say to yourself, twice: 'I am relaxing the muscles in the nape of my neck' ... and do it.

22 Say to yourself, twice: 'I am relaxing the muscles in my back' ... and do it.

23 Say to yourself, twice: 'I am relaxing the muscles in my pelvis' ... and do it.

24 Say to yourself, *three times*: 'I am relaxing the muscles throughout my body' ... and do it.

25 Deepen the feeling of relaxation by imagining yourself in the countryside (by the sea or in the mountains, whatever you like) and yourself resting there or walking, enjoying the delights of the open air, and so on.

Useful tips

The twenty-five steps must be learned in stages:

- in the first lesson, learn steps 1 and 2;
- in the second lesson, revise the first two steps, then learn up to and including step 9;
- in lesson three, revise the nine earlier steps, and learn step 10;
- in lesson four, add step 11 to the others;
- in lesson five, include all 25 steps.

So, to familiarise yourself with this technique, you will need five consecutive lessons, only moving on to the next after you have totally mastered the step or steps included in the first.

When you have thoroughly learned all 25 steps, you must practise them in their entirety, on a regular basis, preferably daily (once you have mastered the technique, this should take less than five minutes).

When you finish, it is recommended that you say, three or four times, 'My body and mind have been strengthened as a result of this session' . . . and so genuinely convince yourself that they have been!

It is only necessary to practise this technique lying down at the beginning. Once you can do all the exercises without the slightest difficulty, and quickly – that is, automatically – you will gradually find that you can practise them sitting or even standing.

30 The Autogenic Training Technique

When to use: for all the problems listed on pp. 25–6.

To end the Techniques section, here is the technique that is universally the best known and the one most often recommended by the medical profession. Autogenic training was developed in the 1920s by J. H. Schultz, a Berlin psychotherapist. Some regard it as 'typically hypnotic', others categorise it simply as a relaxation technique, without mentioning 'hypnosis' or 'self-hypnosis'; but here we are not going to follow the ins and outs of such a debate, which is concerned only with theoretical aspects of the method.

Step-by-step guide

1 Lie on your back or sit comfortably in an armchair, if possible away from any noise, and close your eyes.
2 Say to yourself, in your mind: 'I am absolutely calm' ... and convince yourself that you are.
3 Still in your mind, say to yourself: 'I can feel an irresistible heaviness in my right arm' (in my left arm,

if you are left-handed), and repeat this sentence five times, letting yourself go along with the idea that there is an invisible weight that is making your arm abnormally heavy.

4 When you can really feel that your arm is heavy, fold your arms, breathe deeply and open your eyes.

5 Immediately, shut your eyes again and say to yourself: 'I am absolutely calm,' then add, 'I can feel an irresistible heaviness in my left arm' (right arm, if you are left-handed); repeat this last sentence five times and, as previously, try to convince yourself that what you have said is true.

6 Once you can feel the heaviness of the second arm, say to yourself again: 'I am absolutely calm,' then repeat five times, 'I can feel an irresistible heaviness in my arms and legs,' and try to imagine that your arms and legs are heavy, very heavy . . .

7 When you have succeeded in imagining a great heaviness in your arms and legs, bend them all at the same time, breathe deeply and open your eyes.

8 Close your eyes again and once more say to yourself: 'I am absolutely calm' (and really think it!), then add, 'I can feel an irresistible heaviness in my whole body,' and repeat this sentence five times, using the power of your imagination to feel this sensation of heaviness throughout your body.

9 Once you have experienced the feeling of heaviness in your whole body, allow yourself to relax for a few moments, then fold your arms together, breathe deeply and open your eyes . . .

After this first exercise, which provides excellent relaxation for your muscles, the next exercise, which is for vascular relaxation, involves almost the same procedure, except that this time the sensation that you are seeking is not heaviness in the body but warmth.

1 Find a comfortable position, either lying down or sitting, and if possible away from any noise, and close your eyes.

2 Tell yourself that you are calm, and persuade yourself that you are.

3 In your mind, repeat five times: 'I can feel a pleasant warmth in my left arm (or right arm, if you are left-handed) and using your imagination, feel this warmth.

4 Fold your arms, breathe deeply and open your eyes.

5 Close your eyes again and tell yourself that you are calm . . . and don't lie!

6 Say to yourself, five times: 'I can feel a pleasant warmth in my right arm (or left arm, if you are left-handed), and do your best to feel this in reality.

7 Say to yourself: 'I am absolutely calm' . . . and be so.

8 Say to yourself: 'I can feel a pleasant warmth in my arms and legs,' repeating this four or five times and allowing this imaginary warmth gradually to infiltrate your arms and legs.

9 Fold your arms and breathe deeply, then open your eyes.

10 Close your eyes and say to yourself (with conviction): 'I am absolutely calm.'

11 Say to yourself, five times: 'I can feel a pleasant warmth throughout my entire body' . . . and let this sensation permeate your body.

12 Savour this general feeling of warmth for a few moments.

13 Fold your arms, breathe deeply and open your eyes.

The third exercise is intended to regulate the heartbeat and has only five steps:

1 As in the first two exercises, you must begin by making yourself as comfortable as possible, either lying on your back or sitting in an armchair; then close your eyes.

2 Say to yourself: 'I am absolutely calm' . . . and be aware that you are.
3 Say to yourself: 'My heartbeat is calm and strong.' Repeat this affirmation five times, one after the other, and concentrate, so that you can follow the 'calm, strong' beat of your heart.
4 For a few moments let yourself be lulled by the regular beating of your heart, which you have succeeded in detecting.
5 Fold your arms, breathe deeply and open your eyes.

The three remaining exercises are intended to regulate the respiratory, abdominal and cephalic organs, in that order.

The procedure is identical to that used for regulating the heartbeat, but instead of saying 'My heartbeat is calm and strong', you must, in step 3 of the exercise, say five times:

- 'My lungs are breathing deeply and regularly' for the fourth exercise.
- 'My solar plexus is flooded with a pleasant warmth' for the fifth exercise.
- 'My forehead is permeated with a pleasant coolness' for the sixth exercise . . .

In each case it is essential that you succeed in convincing yourself that you really are experiencing this sensation.

Useful tips

It normally takes about six months to learn autogenic training properly. But if you really apply yourself, you can sometimes learn it in three months, provided you devote the same times, twice a day, to:

- the first exercise (the feeling of heaviness), for fifteen days;
- the second exercise (the feeling of warmth), for fifteen days;

- the third exercise (the heart), for fifteen days;
- the fourth exercise (breathing), for fifteen days;
- the fifth exercise (the solar plexus), for fifteen days;
- the sixth exercise (the forehead), for fifteen days . . .

From this you can see that it is essential not to move on to the next exercise before you have mastered the first, and to know the second thoroughly before you pass on to the third, and so on.

After all this, you can practise all six exercises regularly (once a day) as a kind of daily physical routine. What you will gain for the price of this is a constant balance of body and mind, despite the problems that you may have to face.

If the goal you are seeking is a specialised one (fighting a particular illness, or tiredness, insomnia and so on), there is nothing wrong in confining these exercises (in part or in their entirety) to just one period of time, which can be of variable length, and, if necessary, doing them several times a day.

You should also bear in mind that, despite appearances, autogenic training does not demand that you devote an inordinate amount of time to it; once you have mastered the technique you can do all these exercises in less than quarter of an hour . . .

One final comment: don't take short cuts! As regards the generalised sensation of heaviness or warmth, for example, far from insisting on achieving them right from the beginning, you will have to be patient and wait for them to manifest themselves, after several sessions.

The Tests

When we want to find out whether or not someone is ready to practise self-hypnosis, tests have only a relative value. Quite simply, this is because the 'trigger mechanism' mentioned earlier (see p. 31) also has an important role to play here: it is not uncommon to get a negative result from a test or tests one moment, and the next for the same person to have no problem at all putting him- or herself into a state of self-hypnosis.

On the other hand, the tests are of interest if you want to get some idea of the depth that has been reached in a self-hypnotic state, or if there are times when you would like to obtain 'concrete proof' of self-hypnosis.

The eyelid test

This is the test most frequently used in medical circles. The hypnotherapist will suggest to the patient who has his eyes shut:

'Imagine that you can't open your eyes any more. Close your eyelids tightly . . . I'm going to help you . . .'

Using the thumb and index finger of his right hand, the hypnotist grasps the skin at the top of the patient's nose and continues:

'Your eyes are going to feel heavy . . . Your eyelids will become heavy, very heavy . . . From this moment, your eyelids seem heavy . . . Your eyelids seem heavy . . . Your eyelids are heavy and are becoming heavier and heavier . . . Soon you will no longer be able to open your eyes . . . Even now, your eyelids are stuck together . . . They are stuck faster and faster . . . Opening your eyes will be very difficult for you . . . You will find it incredibly difficult to open your eyes . . . I am sealing your eyes . . . You are no longer able to lift your eyelids and, in a few moments, in spite of all your efforts, it will be impossible for you to open your eyes . . . The muscles in your eyes have contracted . . . With every second that passes, your eyelids are becoming more and more firmly stuck together . . . When I say "three", it will be impossible for you to open your eyes . . . When I say "three", your eyelids will be tightly shut . . . The more you try to raise your eyelids, the less you will be able to do so . . . At "three" it will be impossible for you to open your eyes . . . One . . . Your eyelids are totally fixed . . . Two . . . Your eyelids are stuck more and more firmly . . . Your eyelids are glued together . . . Your eyelids are glued together . . . Three! . . .'

The patient's skin is suddenly released, after which the suggestion reaches its conclusion:

'Now your eyes are fixed . . . You can no longer open them . . . They are stuck together even more firmly . . . They are so firmly glued that you can't open your eyes . . . It's impossible for you to raise your eyelids . . . The more you try to open your eyes, the less you can . . . So try to open them . . . It's impossible, you are incapable of opening your eyes . . . There is a force keeping your eyes closed.'

The gripped hands test

The patient is invited to hold his or her hands together, then the hypnotist says to him or her:

'Hold your hands out in front of you . . . Grip one hand

in the other . . . Grip them even tighter . . . At the same time, straighten your arms and make them rigid, like two steel bars . . . Your hands are attached to each other . . . imagine that your hands are attached as though they have been stuck together with superglue . . . Your hands are stuck together . . . Your hands are stuck together more and more firmly . . . Soon, when I say "three", you won't be able to separate them . . . The more you try to separate them, the more strongly they will become attached to each other . . . The more you try the less you will be able to separate them . . . When I say "three", when you try to separate your hands, you will have the impression that they have fused together . . . You will find it impossible to separate them . . . It will be impossible to undo your hands . . . The more you try to separate them, the more tightly joined they will feel . . . Your arms are becoming more and more rigid . . . Your muscles are contracting . . . Your clenched hands are becoming hard, hard like blocks of wood . . . I am going to count . . . One . . . Your hands are completely fixed . . . Two . . . Your hands are even more firmly stuck together . . . still more . . . They are riveted together . . . They are nailed together . . . They are glued together . . . They are welded together . . . They are gripping each other . . . They are riveted . . . glued . . . welded . . . Three! You are now incapable of separating your hands . . . The more you try, the less you can . . . Your hands are clamped tighter and tighter to each other . . . are riveted together more and more . . . are welded together more and more . . . It is impossible for you to separate your hands . . . imposs-ible . . . The more you try to separate your hands, the tighter they are fixed together. Your hands are un-de-tach-a-ble . . . With every second that passes, your hands are clamped tighter and tighter . . . They are growing into one another . . . It's impossible to undo them . . . Try again . . . You won't succeed . . . Your hands are clamped together, doubly . . . triply . . .'

The weightless arm test

The patient sits or lies down opposite the hypnotherapist who gazes fixedly at him or her, straight in the eyes, saying:

'Imagine that your left arm is going to rise horizontally, until it reaches the height of your face . . . Already, although you can't feel it, your arm is beginning to rise . . . Little by little, your arm is rising . . . More and more, your arm is rising . . . Imagine a fairground . . . You are buying a dozen multicoloured balloons and attaching them to your left wrist . . . The balloons are pulling at your arm . . . They are attached to your wrist and they are pulling your arm upwards . . . As the balloons rise up into the air, your arm is going up as well . . . Dragged by the balloons, your left arm is rising . . . it's rising higher and higher . . . The other arm is staying still, but the one with the balloons is climbing, climbing . . . climbing higher and higher . . . It's become as light as a balloon, your left arm is going up all on its own, higher and higher . . . It's rising . . . it's rising . . . and continuing to rise . . . Higher and higher . . . the balloons are rising, they are dragging your arm with them . . . Your arm is rising, like the balloons, irresistibly . . . It's as light as a balloon . . . your arm is rising . . . rising . . . rising . . . '

The heavy legs test

The patient stands, arms by his or her sides, and is given the following suggestion:

'Imagine that your feet are heavy . . . so heavy that you can't lift them . . . Push your feet against the ground . . . still more . . . Carry all your weight in your feet . . . Imagine that an invisible weight has entered your feet . . . Already your feet seem heavy to you . . . heavier and heavier . . . An invisible weight has slipped into your feet and made them heavy . . . terribly heavy . . . Your feet are getting heavier and heavier and are going to get heavier still . . . Your feet are heavy . . . heavy . . . heavy . . . With every passing second your feet are becoming heavier and heavier . . . heavy . . . heavy . . . And now this heaviness is beginning to spread up your legs . . . More and more . . . your calves are becoming heavy . . . heavy . . . heavy . . . The heaviness is mounting . . . Your feet are heavy, your calves are heavy, and now your thighs are beginning to get heavy, too . . . The muscles in your thighs are contracting . . . Your thighs are becoming stiff . . . Your legs are becoming stiff . . . as stiff as posts . . . Your feet are riveted to the ground . . . your feet are fixed to the ground . . . Your feet are welded to the ground . . . are glued to the ground . . . Your feet are glued to the ground more and more . . . In a moment, when you try to raise them, you won't be able to . . . The more you try, the less you will be able to . . . When I say "three", it will be impossible for you to lift your feet . . . When I say "three", it will be impossible for you to move your legs . . . When I say "three", it will be impossible for you to move forwards or backwards . . . I am going to count . . . One . . . Your feet are heavy, heavy, heavier and heavier, terribly heavy . . . It's as though you had an enormous weight in your feet . . . an enormous weight which is preventing them from moving . . . Two . . . Your feet are even heavier . . . terribly heavy . . . Your feet are riveted to the ground . . . glued to the ground . . . thoroughly glued . . . completely glued to the ground . . . nailed to the ground . . . Three! . . . It's impossible to lift your feet . . . Lifting your feet is absolutely impossible . . . Your feet are too heavy . . . too heavy . . . The more you try to move your feet, the less you can . . . Your legs are so heavy that it's impossible for you to move them . . . Your feet are glued to the ground . . . Your feet are heavy . . . glued to the ground . . . completely glued to the ground . . . It's impossible to go forwards or backwards . . . You are glued, nailed to the ground . . . nailed to the ground . . . It's impossible to move . . . The more you try to move, the more your feet are glued to the ground . . .'

Insensitivity test

The patient is invited to repeat the following, several times:

'My left (right) hand is insensitive to pain . . .'

Then the doctor will pinch the patient's fingers to verify whether or not the suggestion has worked . . .

*   *   *

Note that all these tests are intended to find out whether a self-hypnotic state has been reached, or how deep the state is, and are derived from procedures that are used in hypnotherapy, sometimes to test how susceptible a patient is to hypnosis, sometimes as an aid to inducing hypnosis.

The gripped hands test, the weightlessness test and the insensitivity test can also be done without the help of a hypnotherapist (the person practising the self-hypnosis says to him- or herself: 'My hands are attached to each other . . .' or 'My arm will rise . . .' and so on).

It is also worth mentioning the following point: no matter which of the tests you choose from those described in the previous pages, as a general rule you can assume it has failed if the person is unable to sink into a self-hypnotic state and therefore does not respond to the hypnotist's suggestions. But it goes without saying that this incapacity may only be temporary.

The Awakening

When describing Techniques 27 and 28, we alluded to the procedures that a qualified hypnotherapist uses to end a self-hypnotic state in his patient. It remains for us to tell you how to do this when you are alone.

Well, it couldn't be easier. All you have to do is repeat, three or four times:

'Now I am coming out of self-hypnosis . . . I am waking up.'

'Disguised' awakening

Sometimes, while still in a state of self-hypnosis, you would love to be able to open your eyes and go about your tasks with a greater efficiency than normal, using the constructive attitude you have acquired during the session. In this case, you must suggest to yourself several times:

'As soon as I open my eyes, my self-hypnosis will be even deeper . . .'

Case Histories

Now that you know the different ways to achieve self-hypnosis, or a similarly relaxed state, it is time for a closer look at the benefits it can bring you.

Here are some case histories that will demonstrate how the thirty techniques we have discussed can help you.

Stress

Needs will vary, so sometimes one of the simplest techniques of relaxation can protect you against stress, whereas at other times you may need proper self-hypnosis, as the following case histories will demonstrate.

A knife to the throat

Mme Anne-Marie F., aged 36, had this to say:

'I'm a teacher in a school for children with special needs. This means that I must never lose my temper. There's no question of my letting off steam and raising my voice. The children must always see me with a smile on my face and in a good mood. It's reassuring for them and puts them at their ease. Being extremely sensitive, they tend to get upset easily, so I have to have superhuman patience. It's terribly difficult . . .

'I live quite a long way from my work, and what with the Métro and the bus, it takes me nearly an hour to get to work most mornings. It's even worse going home in the evenings. Sometimes the bus is held up in a traffic jam for at least half an hour. Then there's a hellish journey, jam-packed, on the Métro. The moment I get home I have to prepare dinner – I'm lucky that my husband does the shopping as he finishes work a bit earlier than I do – and then, normally, after our meal, I ought to be able to relax . . .

'Except that for the last eight months we have had unbelievable neighbours, whose only way of communicating with each other is by shouting. It never stops. Husband, wife, mother-in-law, three children – one's still a baby – they're all at it, screaming . . . shouting . . . And that's not all. Even till very late into the night, they have their radio blasting forth; it's tuned in to some foreign station, with this awful monotonous music that keeps me awake, or if I do manage to drop off, it wakes me up.

'We've tried to reason with them, but they take no notice. Now we've had to go to the police about it. They called in the head of the family and, for a few days, we had a bit of peace. But then, one morning, my husband was going downstairs on his way to work, and this stranger stopped him and held a knife to his throat. He said, "If you go on screwing up my friend, if you go back to the police, I'll come and kill you!"

'That same day they started up again. My husband was determined to call the authorities in spite of the threat. I persuaded him not to. Now all we can do is move. Unfortunately the flat we've seen won't be free for another three months, so I've got to find some way of putting up with the way things are until then. I can't go on any longer, I'm so stressed out, I think I'll have a breakdown . . .'

Once she was under hypnosis, the patient was given suggestions that would give her, on the one hand, immediate peace of mind and, on the other, the strength to get through the trials of the coming months, backed up by self-hypnosis. She was taught Technique no. 27 for this.

In addition, so that the patient could have some moments of relaxation before she was able to benefit fully from the effects of Technique 27, she was also taught Technique no. 4.

The combination of the two methods had the desired

effect: she did not succumb to a nervous breakdown as she had feared, and she coped very well as she waited to leave her flat which had become a living hell.

To resign or not to resign: that is the question

Vivianne S., aged 40, described her situation like this:

'For almost four years I had a lover, who's now left me. He said that he no longer felt the passionate love he had once had, and thought of me more as a sister, and so making love was now out of the question . . . It's been a terrible shock, I can tell you.

'Anyway, I'd only just begun to get back on my feet when I had a problem with an inheritance, which put me in a tricky situation. I found I had to fight, I had to turn against several people in my own family who were trying to do me down. It's still not sorted out . . . we're still squabbling . . .

'But what is most painful of all is that at my office there's an atmosphere that's enough to drive you potty. There's a rumour that they are going to "rationalise" on staff. And there are lots of intrigues, with everybody trying to be seen in the best light – it's almost impossible not to get involved . . .

'I'm doing my best to hold on, but I feel I'm losing my grip more and more. I live in a constant state of tension and the situation is getting worse day by day. I'm on the point of giving in my notice, it's that bad – I've just had enough. The only thing that stops me is that I'm afraid I won't get another job easily. It's a risk I daren't take, because I bought a flat last year and the mortgage is quite high. I have to find the money every month for another six years yet . . .'

Vivianne began practising self-hypnosis, using Technique no. 28, and after two weeks she was saying:

'It's definitely much better. I don't take any notice any

more of the bitchy way people behave at the office. I just get on with my job to the best of my ability, and to hell with the rest . . . Nothing gets me into a temper any more. I feel good, really good.'

A man at the end of his tether

George P., aged 59, explained:

'I head an artists' agency that specialises in organising gala events and tours. The people I deal with in the music industry are mostly established stars, and consequently very demanding. I always have to be hard at it, I have to move around a lot, both in this country and abroad.

'More and more my life is becoming a race against the clock, and I have three women to look after. There's my mother who's in hospital, my wife who, deep down, I love dearly, and then there's my mistress who's expecting my child . . .

'So you see I'm in a corner. My professional obligations and my private life don't leave me any time to do any sport or to relax in any other way. And yet I'm in such a state, I think I'll crack up from one day to the next.

'My friends have advised me to take up yoga or autogenic training. They say they work wonders. But I've neither the time nor the patience . . . I must be able to do something simple and easy, which doesn't require months and months to learn . . .'

Just one session of hypnosis was enough for the patient to experience the kind of relaxation he could enjoy through self-hypnosis. I recommended him to use Technique no. 25 and he agreed . . .

The last news I had from him was that he still had the same busy lifestyle, without any breaks, but he was managing to avoid the stress that had almost 'scuppered' him two years before.

An 'infernal' triangle

Jean-Pierre L., aged 42, told me:

'I think I'm going mad. An "infernal" triangle is driving me crazy! Crazier and crazier! . . .

'You see, doctor, I'm so disgusted with the way things stand that I've just about had enough. In the eighteen years we've been together, I've always managed to get by. My wife has never known anything about my infidelities. But now along comes Brigitte, my last conquest to date . . . Can you imagine, instead of immediately destroying one of the letters I sent her *poste restante*, the silly woman had her head stuffed with romantic notions and kept it . . . And, of course, her husband found it!

'That's what started it all. Her husband hired a private detective who managed to track me down, and since then it's been hell. Because that fool wasn't satisfied with just coming to see me and threatening to break my legs, he also decided to tell *my* wife everything . . .

'For the last three months I've had no let-up. Brigitte is besieging me with appeals to start a new life with her. I'm being constantly harassed by her deceived husband, who says if I don't finish with Brigitte, he'll kill me. As for my wife, she just keeps on and on: "I'll kill myself if you go on seeing that woman!"

'Up until last week, I managed to meet Brigitte for an hour at lunchtime. Now that's finished. Not content with coming to meet me at the office at six o'clock, so that she doesn't let me out of her sight till the following morning, my wife's now taken time off work so that she can keep an eye on me at midday as well.

'Since it's not possible to see Brigitte now, even for a brief moment, *she's* taken to telephoning me even at the house. If my wife answers, all Brigitte does is beg her to give me my freedom . . . If she does manage to get through to me, all I get are reproaches . . .

'Her husband's angrier than ever. And with good reason.

Brigitte has told him that she loves me, and that if I decide to, we're going to live together. "It only needs one word from you and I'll leave," she's threatening him. So he's always on the phone too, raving like a lunatic – sometimes he gets my wife, sometimes he gets me . . .

'So you can see, I've got my wife on one side and Brigitte and her deceived husband on the other tormenting me night and day. It's not surprising I'm going off my head.

'And at the office I'm making silly mistakes all day long, and if that goes on I'll be out of a job . . .

'I know I should just ignore everything that's happening, but it's impossible to concentrate on my work. I do try, but my mind's always somewhere else . . . Even if, on rare occasions, I do manage to get through a whole hour without my wife or Brigitte or her husband phoning me, I can still hear them in my head . . .'

A session of hypnosis gave this patient immediate relief. I then advised him to relax several times a day whether he was at work or at home, by using Techniques 1 or 2 (depending on the circumstances) and at the same time to learn Technique no. 29 to rid himself entirely of the tension caused by the 'infernal' triangle . . .

As he gradually regained his ability to concentrate, Jean-Pierre L. avoided dismissal. As for his private life, the three techniques he used enabled him to enjoy a mental state in which he could reflect and make important decisions. And, in the end, he decided not to see his mistress any more, but also to separate from his wife, at least to give him time to think straight.

My car, my love

Lionel F., aged 55, confided in me:

'I suppose it's ridiculous to attach so much importance to such things. But I can't help it. It's stronger than I am, I love beautiful things, I surround myself with beautiful objects, and when I look at them, I forget any problems at work, I feel happy. My Regency furniture, the few pictures I have, all by little-known artists but very talented ones nonetheless, and my collection of Art Deco glass – they're all a consolation if my day's gone badly at work, which happens quite a lot.

'My car's the same. I fell in love with the beauty of its line and its harmonious proportions. I bought it solely because of that. It's a Triumph Spitfire – they're not made any more – and I've had it almost twenty years. Finding spare parts is becoming more and more difficult but I still manage to keep it in perfect working order. As for the bodywork, apart from having it completely resprayed every so often, I make sure it's always immaculate so that it's a pleasure to look at.

'Up until last spring everything was going relatively well, because there was a garage in the apartment block where I lived. Unfortunately, when the recession set in, I had to move. The rent I pay at the moment isn't too bad, but there's no garage, so I have to park my Spitfire in the street. It's what you might call a rough neighbourhood, so, not surprisingly, almost every morning I find my car's been tampered with in some way. Sometimes it's the hubcaps that have been stolen, sometimes the hood's been damaged, or someone's run a knife along the bonnet or the doors – there's always something. I don't know if you can imagine what I feel each time. In fact, I'm furious. It's like an obsession. I think about it all the time, wherever I am. And I have the most appalling nightmares. Which is understandable because every time I go to bed, I'm worrying in case there's more vandalism in the night.

'You'll probably tell me the only solution is to change my car and make do with something less conspicuous, less provocative. But I just can't resign myself to that. I love my beautiful old Spitfire so much! No, I can't do it, I won't part with it. All I want, you see, is just to become a bit more thick-skinned. It would be good if I could just accept that parts *are* going to be stolen and the bodywork damaged without making such a drama out of it. It would be good if I weren't so stressed all the time because I'm so apprehensive about the damage to my car.'

I advised my patient to practise Technique no. 9 daily, morning and evening for at least three weeks. But in fact, after ten days, he told me:

'You could say these exercises have been a success. Just imagine, yesterday morning I found my Spitfire with the rear right wing scratched, and I didn't turn a hair! I now find myself waiting with a certain detachment to see what the hit-and-run drivers and the vandals will be up to next.'

General Health

Here are some typical case histories to illustrate what self-hypnosis can do towards:

- preventing different kinds of illness;
- curing psychosomatic ailments;
- alleviating or killing pain;
- curbing overeating, smoking addiction and alcoholism;
- curing insomnia.

A flirt

Anne G., aged 27, was very prone to respiratory infections – she had already had pneumonia, bronchitis (a number of times) and laryngitis, but she made no secret of her problem:

'I like to please. So when it's nice weather or even in midwinter, I do a stupid thing. I know I shouldn't, it only needs a small draught for me to catch cold, but I do like wearing low-cut dresses . . .'

Under hypnosis, the patient's resolve to be more sensible was reinforced. I also recommended her to practise Technique no. 29, so that the self-hypnosis would help prevent her changing her mind.

The result: Anne G. managed to control her inborn coquetry. Thereafter she abstained from all sartorial imprudence, and so avoided catching chills.

A gourmand

Michael B., aged 54, often suffered from liver problems and complained:

'It's terrible. I can control my eating at home, but the moment I'm out with friends or with a client in a restaurant, I eat enough for four and drink like a fish . . .'

We decided on a method that could be used immediately, since the patient was exposing himself to the dangers of overindulgence. This was Technique no. 27. Michael B. learned how to put himself under self-hypnosis by using a keyword – in his case it was 'sober' – which he would use to put himself into a state in which he would no longer succumb to gastronomic temptations . . .

And, as a result, the 'incriminating' business lunches or dinners with friends ceased to end in bilious attacks.

False alarm

Robert S., who was 37 and had a chronic skin complaint, recalled:

'It all began about ten years ago when I spent the night with a woman who was working for UNESCO. While we were making love, I noticed she kept on scratching herself. That worried me. In fact it worried me very much. I wondered if it had anything to do with postings she had had in the Third World . . . On the other hand, I tried to reassure myself. I told myself that she came from a good family and had a number of university degrees, and anyway she wasn't the type of woman who . . .

'However, the next day I had pimples, all over my neck, chest and genitals. And it all itched unbearably. The

150

consultant I saw took a skin sample and gave me some ointment . . . which gave me no relief at all. Then I had to go to a laboratory for a blood sample to be taken.

'The week after, I went back to the dermatologist. He told me that if the tests were to be believed, there was nothing wrong with me . . . "But, you know, in our branch of medicine," he said, "there are still a lot of gaps . . . It could be that your problem is purely and simply psychosomatic . . ."

'I can't remember now what medication was prescribed after the tests, but the fact is that it was all as useless as the ointment.

'For about two months I made myself remain celibate. And gradually, everything went back to normal. But since then, one time in two, when I have a new relationship, it starts up all over again: a few hours after the first time we have sex, the pimples come back.

'I wanted to be clear in my own mind, so I had other tests done three weeks ago. Still nothing. It's not AIDS, or anything else . . .'

It seemed obvious that the first appearance of the symptom came from the fear of contracting a contagious disease (venereal or otherwise). Then afterwards, in similar situations, that is whenever the healthiness of his partner raised doubts, it automatically unleashed a new crop of pimples . . .

Technique no. 28 was offered to this patient as a suitable means of combating his fears. And with the help of this form of self-hypnosis, his problem never returned.

Those irresistible cakes

Annie T., who was 32, was worried by her binge-eating. She explained:

'I'm an accountant for an advertising company, which has recently opened a branch in Belgium. Once a month, I have to spend five days at a time in Brussels, to see to our office's accounts there . . . and the office happens to be right next to one of the best pâtisseries in the city.

'I have to confess I've always adored sweet things. But, happily for me, I've gradually managed to wean myself off our own pastries. Weeks can pass without my eating any, and even now I can manage to go without any of the things sold in our own pâtisseries.

'But in Brussels, just looking at those wonderful cakes, piled with whipped cream and all the other glorious confections, immediately makes my mouth begin to water. I just have to have them. They're just so incredibly delicious, I can't resist them.

'Every time I have to be there, instead of going to a restaurant for my midday meal, I visit that wonderful pâtisserie and all caution goes to the winds. Between Monday and Friday, I average three and four cakes a day, and by the end of the week I've put on another five pounds or more. It makes no difference if, for the rest of the month when I'm not working in Belgium, I give up all sweet things; the damage is done and I'm finding it more and more difficult to lose all that extra weight . . .'

Annie began to use Technique no. 11, and through it became more moderate in her eating habits: now, when she stays in Brussels, she only eats one cake a day and so doesn't put on any extra weight.

The sword of Damocles

Pierre O., aged 54, suffered from chronic bronchial asthma:

'My sole reason for coming to see you, doctor, is because my daughter insisted on it. She's a great believer in alternative medicine . . . Quite frankly, I can't say I have any faith in any sort of treatment any more. I've seen a number of doctors and senior consultants. I've taken goodness knows how many types of medication and still am . . . but nothing seems to make the situation any better . . .'

As we went further into the interview, I learned that about twelve years previously, and some six months before his first attack, Pierre had almost been killed on a building site. Since that accident, he had never felt totally safe, even in the most secure situations, but he was still determined to go on working in the building trade, though every morning he would say to himself: 'Maybe today I'll get killed . . .'

Two sessions of hypnosis helped Pierre overcome his scepticism and first learn, then practise, Technique no. 30. As recommended by Schultz (the man to whom we owe autogenic training) he prolonged the time he took to expel his breath (counting up to ten), and extended the suggestion of feeling a sensation of coolness in his forehead to his eyes and throat; he also concentrated on the suggestion of feeling a sensation of warmth in his chest.

Gradually Pierre O. managed to overcome his feelings of apprehension, and it wasn't long before his attacks began to get less frequent. At the beginning of the second year after he had begun practising Technique no. 30 on a daily basis, he ceased to have any bronchial asthma at all.

On the move

Jocelyne A., aged 34, suffered from high blood pressure.

'I have to be on the move all the time. I couldn't imagine myself working in an office or a shop. You see, my husband and I work for a domestic electrical appliance factory. We have to give sales demonstrations at all the large fairs and shows, so we're on the road all the time. We've been doing it for the last five years and I love it.

'Last spring, in spite of the pill, I still don't know how it happened . . . anyway I'm expecting a baby this coming December and my gynaecologist has told me that I shall have to stop, otherwise I'm likely to run into a lot of trouble . . .

'I'm not worried about looking after the baby, especially

153

as my mother can care for it when the time comes, but it's the time between now and then . . . You see, if I take maternity leave, the company will want to replace me, and my husband will have to work with some other woman. If he sleeps with her I'll go mad, but what I'm afraid of is that this woman will settle into the job and afterwards they'll want to keep her and I'll have to work somewhere else, when I love travelling around! . . . I can't bear the thought!'

Since the patient would always be on the move, it was impossible to help her with regular sessions of hypnosis. We therefore decided on self-hypnosis, using Technique no. 27 to teach it, with the aim of getting rid of the anxiety that had caused her high blood pressure.

Six weeks after the treatment began, Jocelyne A. came back to our office and said:

'I'm not worried any more. I've become fatalistic about things. What will be will be. If the bastards replace me for good, too bad, it won't be the end of the world. From next Monday, I'm taking a rest, and I'll have my baby. After that, we'll see . . .'

And it has to be said that with such a change in her attitude (achieved through self-hypnosis) her blood pressure returned to normal.

Seduced and abandoned

Mireille R., who was 39 years old, was suffering from a duodenal ulcer. She told us:

'I'm desperately unhappy. I used to have a husband who always did his best to make me happy, and I left him for a married man I'd lost my head over. Our affair lasted for seven years. He was all I could have wished for, I won't deny it. But, you see, there came a time when I could only see him once or twice a week, and never at weekends or during the holidays. I begged him to get a divorce, and in the end he said he would. I thought that at last we'd be able

154

to live together. But no, he led me up the garden path for month after month, and then I learned that in fact he was also seeing a girl of 22. So, naturally, I created a scene. And to punish me, not only did he tell me he intended to marry this other girl, but he also chose that moment to tell me that he was tired of me relying on him to make ends meet, and I couldn't count on him any more to help me out.'

Parallel with treatment by hypnosis, the patient also used self-hypnosis. The two procedures helped to lessen her heartache and restore her mental balance, so that she would be able to find a job to keep her going and thus solve her financial problems on her own.

In less than two months Mireille R. managed to stop constantly thinking about her ex-lover's skulduggery and begin to look for a job. With her knowledge of book-keeping, she was able to find an opening with a company that was expanding, and she was taken on, on probation. With regular practice of Technique no. 25, her work was good enough for the company to confirm her appointment, and examination of her duodenal ulcer revealed that it had healed itself.

Enough to make you scream

Roger P., aged 47, suffered from chronic rheumatism in his lower limbs, and explained:

'In the end, what's worst is that when I get my attacks, the pain is so bad I can't help crying out. Anybody who hears me must think I'm raving mad . . .'

Using Technique no. 26, the patient quickly learned to control his pain, and even when he had his worst attacks (brought on by the weather), he was able to go about his business without experiencing again the kind of pain that made him want to scream.

Unbearable

Sophie G., aged 41, complained of migraines:

'Especially when I have my periods, it's absolutely atrocious. I feel as though my head is going to explode into a thousand pieces,' she said. 'It never lasts for very long, but when it does happen, I don't know myself any more, I just want to pack everything in, I'm just unbearable . . . For years and years, I've used aspirin. But now I'm getting side effects and the doctor treating me advised me to stop taking it and to come and see you . . .'

Here again, Technique no. 26 proved to be the answer: using the colour contrast phenomenon, self-hypnosis gave the patient a proper period of respite, which enabled her to ignore the pain altogether at times, and at others to feel it only slightly.

Nightmarish nights

Armand M., who was 53, suffered from renal colic. He told me:

'As far as I'm concerned, I'm reconciled to putting up with this hell, but I have a reason for coming. The problem is that I remarried two years ago and my young wife is beginning to say she's had enough nightmarish nights with me. All my moans and groans, grinding of teeth and twitching are seriously getting on her nerves . . .'

The patient came to see me at a time when he was having one of his attacks. He was advised to use Technique no. 25 to lessen the severity of the pain. At the same time, he was also recommended to learn Technique no. 29, so that, through practising it daily, he would be better prepared to cope with any future attacks. After three months he was able to stop himself reacting outwardly to the extreme pain these attacks invariably produced.

Monster appetite

Fabienne I. was 28 and wanted to stop overeating. She confided:

'I haven't ever been able to exercise any self-control since seeing my mother die slowly and excruciatingly of cancer. The poor thing spent her whole life on a strict diet just to stay slim and healthy . . . But now I weigh 11 stones 5 lb., in other words, I'm almost two stone overweight, and I'm beginning to believe I'll never get back to what I used to weigh. And what's worse, I'm always hungry . . .'

The patient was hypnotised and suggestions given to orientate her towards three goals:

- to convince herself that she could slim;
- to resolve to go on a suitable diet;
- to neutralise the impact of her mother's death and the conclusion she had drawn from it.

The patient was also advised to practise Techniques nos. 11 and 25, to strengthen her ability to avoid the pitfalls that are brought about by greed disguised as 'hunger'.

As a result of this, after seven months, Fabienne I. returned to her normal weight and has well and truly made up her mind never to get fat again.

From one extreme to another

Bernard W., aged 37, wanted to stop smoking, and explained:

'I just went from one extreme to another. Quite possibly, because my parents had never forbidden me to smoke, for years I had no desire to smoke at all, while all my friends always had a cigarette in their mouth, even at junior school, let alone at the lycée.

'Then, when I was about 28, I fell in love with a woman who was a really heavy smoker: two packets a day! . . . It's really stupid, but because of her smoking I got a complex.

So I took it up as well.

'At the beginning, I didn't inhale . . . The main thing was to give the impression that I was on the same wavelength as she, this woman, was . . . I can't even remember her name now.

'You can guess the rest, easily enough. Gradually, I got so that I couldn't carry on without a smoke. I've tried to stop three or four times. I can manage it for a few days, but that's all: then I have to start again.

'Now I'm perfectly aware of the need to stop. I sometimes have memory blocks, I get out of breath more and more easily and the girl I'm living with now doesn't smoke, she can't stand the smell on my breath.

'The problem is that when I have managed to get through an hour or two without lighting up, I get very irritable and even have headaches . . .'

To start with, Technique no. 25 was a considerable help in reducing the number of cigarettes Bernard W. smoked per day (in two months, it went down from twenty to eight or ten at the most). Then the patient also learned Technique no. 29 and practised it daily, and the combination of these two techniques made it possible for him to give up tobacco altogether, six months after the treatment began.

A need to forget

Florence E., aged 40, was an alcoholic, but she defended herself:

'Oh, you know, it's not really serious. One or two scotches when I come home from the office, just to release the tension a bit. I don't know why my friend is making such a meal out of it . . .'

The friend in question had a different version of what happened when Florence came home from the office:

'Every evening, Florence comes home with a bottle of whisky tucked under her arm. At the beginning of our relationship I tried to reason with her. She'd become a fury and break everything. So after a while I stopped interfering.

'So when she gets home, she drinks half a bottle of whisky before dinner, has wine with her meal, then calmly finishes the rest of the whisky watching television. And what effect does it have? Well, she talks about her childhood, her drinking bouts with her mother and stepfather, and also talks about the men she knew before me; then she says all this is getting fuzzier in her mind and that by systematically drinking every evening, she'll be bound to forget it all, and then she'll be able to love me more than ever. Towards midnight she collapses, and I have to help her, otherwise she'd never be able to get into bed. Once she's lying down she makes fantastic love, then suddenly falls asleep and starts snoring . . . and snoring . . .'

Once she was in a state of hypnosis, the patient was invited to reveal the deep reason for her need to 'forget everything' and it was thus that we came to learn of certain traumas she had undergone at the ages of nine, twenty and twenty-eight.

My first aim was to make Florence E. discover the impact hypnotic relaxation could have, so that she could begin to understand that alcohol isn't the only means of finding reassurance.

After the third session of classic hypnosis, the patient was introduced to self-hypnosis, as described in Technique no. 28, and she was advised to practise what she had learned every evening as soon as she got home . . . even before opening the whisky bottle.

With the feeling of well-being that came with the self-hypnosis, coupled with the beneficial effects of the three sessions of hypnosis she had already had, Florence felt less and less need to rush to the whisky bottle. She continued to drink, of course, but gradually the amount she consumed grew less: about a month after the treatment had begun, a bottle would last two nights, and barely a fortnight after that, three nights.

During the third month, a fairly significant aggravation at work caused her to lapse (a bottle an evening again, for three nights in a row) and also caused an interruption in her self-hypnosis.

Fortunately, thanks to her friend's intervention, she agreed to come back to my consulting-rooms for two more sessions of hypnosis, three days apart, to prepare the ground for continuing her own daily sessions of self-hypnosis. The effect, once again, was a gradual diminution of her alcohol intake. And, at the end of seven months, the 'miracle' is that Florence E. is able to manage without whisky; she drinks just a little wine at mealtimes and that's all! . . .

A weakness

Sylvie I. was 41 years old and complained of frequent insomnia:

'There's something annoying me and putting me in such a temper I can't sleep,' she said.

So what was it?

She wasn't keen to say, but I made it clear that it was imperative to know the deep cause for her troubles, so in the end she loosened up.

'I won't have people passing remarks about my hairstyle and make-up and clothes. I've always tried not to be inconspicuous, to make my looks highlight my personality. In the past, no one found cause to say anything, or if they did it was a compliment. Nowadays, more and more people reproach me for being "eccentric" . . . As if only young girls have any right to . . .'

She paused for a while, looking confused, and then began again with a sob:

'I can't bear it any longer! I've never done anyone any harm . . . So why criticise me? Is it such a crime if I forget to look my age?'

The patient was given a session of hypnosis intended to

inoculate her against her colleagues' insinuations. And she was advised, in the form of post-hypnotic suggestion, totally to disregard the opinions of those around her, and to remain true to herself . . .

Parallel to the strong reinforcement of the patient's resolution to ignore the passing years, and to help her sleep, the therapy also included using Technique no. 4.

A fortnight later, Sylvie I. took the trouble to telephone me and joyfully announced:

'Can you imagine, doctor, yesterday one of my colleagues said to me: "Frankly, I wonder how you have the nerve to buy such loud earrings. I wouldn't wear them even if I were in my teens!" Instead of making a scene, I laughed in her face. And I found in the evening that I didn't need to use the method you'd taught me any more, I feel at such peace with myself that I fall asleep the moment my head touches the pillow.'

Justifiable torment

Regis D., aged 57, suffered from insomnia and told me the exact details:

'I go to bed at around eleven or twelve, and two or three hours later I'm still awake. Then, finally I drop off, but after an hour or two I wake up again and spend hours and hours before I finally get to sleep . . .

'I suppose it's not really surprising, since I'm agonising over my wife. She's actually abroad for quite a long time. She telephones me almost every day, and she always says lots of sweet little things to me, but . . . You see, there's a twenty-five-year age-gap between us, so I can't help feeling jealous . . .'

Using Technique no. 23, the patient began to sleep distinctly better.

Two sessions of hypnosis, three days apart, with suggestions intended to neutralise the anxiety that had caused his insomnia, all combined to restore his normal sleep pattern, which returned barely nine days after he had begun the treatment.

Money worries

Suffering from intermittent insomnia, Lucien R, aged 33, told me:

'Shortly after I bought a new car on hire purchase I lost my job. My redundancy payment wasn't enormous, but my unemployment benefit is enough to cover the rent and pay for a few odds and ends. The problem is my car. I make an interim payment when I can. Unfortunately it doesn't happen often . . .'

By practising Technique no. 24, the patient was able to sleep properly even when his instalment payments were late.

Studying and Exams

Self-hypnosis can be a valuable help to students and anyone preparing for exams or tests, but certain similar techniques can also contribute to success.

Overloaded

Anne-Marie M., who was 19, said:

'I don't know what's happened, but I don't seem able to concentrate on my studies any more, I just feel I want to chuck it all. My mother is beside herself, it's she who insisted I come to see you . . .'

Our interview did not stop there, but became more probing, and this was how the problem began to emerge: Anne-Marie M. felt overloaded because, as a victim of the consumer society, she did not have the patience to carry through her studies to the end, she wanted to start to earn her living right away, like her best friend who had found a good job . . . without any qualifications at all!

She went on:

'At the same time, I know it would be stupid if I sulked about it. My mother has sacrificed such a lot for me, her dream has always been that I should have a career in law.' I asked her if she was prepared to make an effort not to make her mother unhappy. She said 'yes', she was, and so I was able to employ a tactic that would help her . . .

Using Technique no. 28, the patient learned how to use self-hypnosis to regain an interest in her studies. She was also advised to practise Technique no. 7 to strengthen her powers of concentration.

As a result, Anne-Marie M. no longer feels drawn to the easy way out, but attends her classes with growing enthusiasm.

In a panic

Jean-Marc B., aged 22, confided:

'The date for my exams is getting nearer and I'm beginning to panic. I'm afraid I'm not up to the mark. Yet I've worked hard. All I need now is to be able to revise everything methodically and calmly. The trouble is I'm not managing to do this . . .'

Using Technique no. 27, and also practising Technique no. 5 on a daily basis, made it possible for Jean-Marc B. to do the necessary revision under proper conditions and to go into his exams without any sign of nerves.

Exhausted

Philippe U, aged 27, explained:

'I work in a factory, because I broke off my studies when I was 15. It's something I regret now. For two months I've been doing evening classes and I would like to go on with them, but I'm already feeling exhausted . . .'

A clinical examination revealed no signs of overwork, leaving me to conclude that the tiredness he felt was purely and simply in the mind. So that he could carry on his project unhindered, the patient was started off with

Technique no. 28, but also shown Technique no. 5 and recommended to practise it daily. And that is how Philippe U. spent his daytime hours doing manual work, and still managed to devote the necessary time to persevering at his studies.

Stagefright

Maryse A., aged 32, complained:

'Every time I have to take a test, I become incapable of showing off my knowledge in the oral, but I have no problems with the written part, which means that so far I've got by. Except that I'm afraid I might fail my final exams, where the orals are more important.'

Using Technique no. 25, the patient was able to overcome her stagefright and passed her exam without difficulty.

Disheartened

Simonne F., aged 28, explained her problem:

'Even when I was very little, I was extremely clever with my hands. I wanted to be a sculptress. But my father wanted me, as his only daughter, to do what he'd done, and have a career in the Higher Civil Service. He was so good at persuading me that I gave up my dream of going to art school and ended up in law school. And once I had my degree, he used his influence to get me a job in the Ministry of Finance. In the end, I could hardly complain. The job was what you might call a "cushy number". When I finished at the office, I was free to spend my time doing things I really wanted to do.

'But, five months ago, my father persuaded me that staying where I was wasn't good enough. Once again, he arranged everything. It seemed I had to sit a further exam, to get promotion. So, for the past few months, what with my work at the ministry, the training course, evening classes and homework, it's been practically impossible to live a normal life.

'At first my boyfriend was supportive. He was very understanding and affectionate – he helped me a lot. Then, from about two months ago, when he became unemployed, our relationship has deteriorated. He has so many worries, and I'm busy with my studies for the exam. On the rare occasions when we can spend an evening together, it always ends badly. We never get round to making love properly any more, we're constantly at each other's throats and quarrelling . . .

'And that's not all. To cheer myself up I've developed a bad habit of nibbling all day. Sweet things, savoury things, anything. And in less than a month I've put on almost eight and a half pounds . . .

'And to crown it all, this blasted exam is becoming harder and harder. The subjects they've given us I find very difficult to follow. In two months we've got the written tests, and the orals a month later. I feel I haven't a hope in hell of passing. I just feel I'm wasting my time and wonder whether it's worth going on with it. In a word, I'm completely disheartened. And yet I must be able to go on. Because my father's so insistent. And if I give up he'll reproach me for it for the rest of my life.'

Simonne agreed to tackle her problems on three fronts. She adopted Technique no. 16 to try to restore the good sexual relationship she had had with her partner. She learned Technique no. 11 to put a quick end to accumulating extra pounds. And finally, to help see her through her exams, she practised Technique no. 6 and Technique no. 9.

Early results: her sexual relationship became satisfying again (after two weeks of daily exercises) and she managed to cut out snacks between her three main meals (she lost over four pounds in three weeks and is continuing the slimming diet she started).

After that, she took up Technique no. 19 to complement

Techniques 6 and 9, and now Simonne F. can concentrate properly on preparing for her exams and it's becoming obvious she will pass.

Distracted

Madeleine O., aged 34, telephoned to ask for an appointment and said:

'This time, it's about my son. He's twelve and his name's Victor. He's an intelligent, sensitive, gentle boy. He's had no problems at school – till now. But he's started bringing home bad reports. His teachers say his attention is wandering – too much – as if he's not interested in his classes any more.'

A couple of days later, neither the deep conversation I had with Victor nor the clinical examination revealed anything wrong, but they did highlight the boy's sensitivity – perhaps excessive sensitivity – that his mother had alluded to. And when the conversation turned towards trying to find the cause of his lack of concentration, the boy revealed:

'I spend my whole time thinking about Roger.'

'Who's Roger?'

'Mummy will tell you.'

I did not press further. Victor might have become more withdrawn, and a few minutes later his mother enlightened me:

'Roger is both my boss and my lover. I was already divorced when I met him. At that time I had no inkling that one day I'd be on intimate terms with him. I respected him and liked him and that's where it stopped. And then, it doesn't matter how, it didn't take me long to discover that one of my colleagues, Florence somebody, was his mistress and that he loved her to distraction.

'Last year Roger had a stroke. Almost immediately, Florence took off abroad with a man who it seems had been in her life for some time. I went to see Roger in hospital every day, and he seemed unable to get over it. It was the worst let-down in his life, he told me, and said he wished the doctors had let him die.

'Even now I'm not sure whether I was motivated just by pity or not. What's certain is that I was absolutely determined Roger should get back his enthusiasm for life. And gradually, as I continued visiting him in hospital, my role as bearer of office news became more and more just a pretext for seeing him. I visited him to give him some human warmth, some tenderness, to prove to him that in spite of his illness and its debilitating after-effects, and also the fact that he was 66, a young and reasonably good-looking woman still found him attractive.

'After a long convalescence, Roger is now doing quite well. Therapy has helped him, although he still can't use his left leg and arm, but his morale is good and his mind is just as lively as it was before he went into hospital. For the last six months we've been living together. He's really fond of Victor and showers him with presents. Victor also seems to have a great affection for him. So, now you know all there is to know about Roger . . .'

Once I knew these details, it was easier to carry on the conversation with the son. I asked him:

'What is it about Roger you don't like?'

'Nothing. He's very kind to me, and to Mummy, he's really nice.'

'And yet, according to what you told me just now, he's the one who's responsible for your lack of interest in your schoolwork. Didn't you say you thought about him all the time?'

'It's Cyril's fault – he's a friend. He came to our house and he saw Roger and Mummy kissing. Ever since, I've been a laughing stock in my class. He told everyone how my mother lived with a man who was on crutches and was so old he could be my grandfather . . .'

To improve Victor's powers of concentration for his schoolwork, I proposed Techniques 5 and 7. To neutralise the ill-effects of his friend Cyril's unthinking remarks, Technique no. 12 was advised.

So, as he waited for admission to a different school (where his fellow pupils would know nothing of his mother's private life), Victor could truly improve his output, even if only gradually . . .

Work in General

Whatever type of work you do, and whether you are male or female, one or other of the techniques we have discussed may help you overcome obstacles you have encountered.

In despair

Pierre S., who is 57, confided:

'With the economic crisis, my situation has become appalling. I'm a professional painter and for the last two years, to all intents and purposes, my income has been nil. My last exhibition to date was eight months ago. Only one of my pictures sold. As usual, the gallery took fifty per cent of the money, and all I had went towards paying four months' back rent.

'I used to have regular commissions for set designs and ballet costumes. From a choreographer friend. But after the change in government, the new man in charge of the relevant department in the Ministry of Culture decided to withdraw the subsidy to the ballet company. Now my friend is working abroad and the theatres there insist on him using their own stage and costume designers.

'I didn't have much luck either when I managed to supplement the irregular sales of my paintings by producing handpainted silk scarves. It went very well for about three years, then the fashion changed and the shop that sold them didn't want them any more.

'Quite recently, I tried to make a go of T-shirts. I decorated them by hand with signs of the Zodiac. Everyone thought they were wonderful. But I've got no head for business, and I never managed to sell them in any great quantity. My friends and acquaintances only bought a few dozen in all. And, more often than not, I wasn't very good at chasing up money that was owed. But anyway they didn't cost much. About 400 francs each (£50) . . . for authentic works of art: some people didn't buy them to wear, they had them framed.

'Nowadays, perhaps more than ever, there are an awful lot of painters who are finding it difficult to live solely from their art, and some don't make it at all. Some have found a way by giving classes or private tuition. Friends suggested that to me, but the trouble is I've no talent for teaching painting. I tried it once or twice a long time ago. It was a disaster.

'I simply don't know which way to turn any more. All I have are debts. And fewer and fewer friends can indulge in buying a painting or even lending me a bit of cash. Almost everyone I know has money problems.

'A voice inside me tells me I should be changing my style and my subject-matter. I would love to do that, I would love to paint a new series of pictures which were totally different from what I'd done before. But logically I think I might be wasting my time, since the situation at the present time isn't favourable to any expansion in the art market. So the days go by with nothing constructive happening. I sleep and sleep, and sleep. I get up late, feed the cat, do some chores and immediately feel so tired that I go back to bed again. In the early evening I force myself to go to a private view. In the vague hope of meeting someone who might be able to get me out of this mess. But, nowadays, collectors and art dealers are not so free with their money as they were twenty or even ten years ago. Before making any purchase, they give it a lot of thought . . .

'In the flat next to mine there's a fellow painter who does pictures that are easy to sell. He doesn't have any worries . . . He's just bought a Porsche. If only I didn't have such high ideals and this need to create something worthy of the name of art, perhaps at this moment I would be in a similar position to him. Only, what's done is done. And, quite honestly, I think that with the personality I have it would have been impossible to compromise again and again, just to earn enough to live on.

'So, I just don't know where I'm heading, I don't know whether it mightn't be better just to put an end to it once and for all. It's not impossible that my usual gallery will offer me a new exhibition, more or less in the near future. But as I've already said, I don't seem able to apply myself to my work. I've no courage left, no inspiration, no will. Just a feeling of despair.'

Techniques no. 13 and 25 were recommended (with the self-hypnotic suggestion: 'I am going to recover my vitality and creativity, and my optimism as well'), and the exercises were to be done several times a day.

About two months after this consultation, Pierre S. rang me:

'I'm gradually managing to get back on my feet. I've begun painting again. Eight paintings . . . in six weeks! They're figurative with an element of fantasy, something that I've never done before. I showed some colour photos of them to some people on the council (I'd actually contacted them about social security). They were enthusiastic. And thanks to their help, I shall soon be having a one-man show at the local town hall. They seem to think I shouldn't have any problem in getting sales.'

Indecision

Isabelle T., aged 34, explained:

'I've only lived in the capital for six years. Before, I taught German (my mother tongue) in a commercial college run by my father in Lille. I decided to change jobs and came to Paris for two reasons. The first was that I wasn't getting on very well with my husband. He has an enormous number of good qualities, but . . . In the end, we didn't divorce, we simply separated and we've stayed really good friends. The second reason was connected with my parents. Their way of thinking is diametrically opposed to mine and along with my husband we all lived in the same house, and if it wasn't him, it was them I was quarrelling with all the time.

'So, one fine day, I took my courage in both hands and packed my bags. Since then I only go back to Lille for the odd weekend. As a general rule, I also go there at Easter, and at the end of the year, and for part of my summer holidays. I do it so that I can be near my grandmother, who's a darling, the person I love most in the whole world.

'I found my job in the classified ads. In a travel agency in Paris. They needed someone who could speak fluent German as well as English. After the usual probationary period, I was put in charge of a section that specialised in trips to German-speaking countries.

'Like all our competitors, we suffered as a result of the Gulf War. Three of my colleagues were made redundant last year. I half expected my turn was coming, and, sure enough, it came almost a year ago too. And my father immediately suggested I should go back to work for him. I refused. I went on the dole, I took evening classes and training courses, like everyone else looking for work. At the same time I contacted all the German, Austrian and Swiss companies with whom I'd had excellent relations during the five years I'd worked at the agency. One of them, whose main office was in Vienna, offered me the possibility of working with them, with me as a sort of French agent for them.

'I had to do some research, then try to get organised tours off the ground. Everything was done to help me. Really, those Austrians were marvellous, they trusted me completely. Unfortunately, after six months I'd not managed to complete a single item of business. Every time, just at the last moment – it didn't make any difference whether it was a public or a private organisation I'd been negotiating intensely with over weeks and weeks – they'd end up cancelling their reservations for this or that tour in Austria. Sometimes it was because they'd just received a more interesting quotation than ours, sometimes because they hadn't got sufficient bookings.

'As a result, I'm back where I started: still out of work. Every approach I've made so far to companies connected directly or indirectly with tourism has come to nothing. It seems that my ambition to stay in the travel industry is insurmountably blocked.

'Of course I could still go back to my old profession. In theory, I wouldn't have too much difficulty finding a post in a language school. But I wonder whether I could re-adjust to the monotonous way of life . . .

'You see, I'm a Sagittarian. Which means I adore travel. When I worked for the agency it was marvellous, I often had to go abroad with my job, and I could get cut-price air tickets to just about anywhere in the world for my holidays. The Far East, America, Australia, South Africa, I went everywhere. Often I would get invitations from hotels or tourist organisations and I could spend breaks entirely free of charge in exotic places. All that would be finished if I went back to teaching.

'On the other hand, soon I won't have any more unemployment benefit, or anyway, not enough. As you know, rents have gone up quite a lot in Paris. If I don't get a job soon I shall have to dip into my savings, and whatever I do, they won't keep me going for long.

174

'Only a couple of days ago, my father phoned me again to find out if I was ready to join up with his team again. He wants a reply before the end of next week. If I turn it down he'll take on someone else. I just can't make up my mind. Should I go back to Lille? Look for work in Paris as a teacher? Continue the struggle till I find a job in tourism again? . . . My mind's in a turmoil. I can't think, I can't reach a point where I can choose properly. I'm just dithering . . .'

For Isabelle T., to give her some peace of mind that would enable her to take a detached view of her anxieties and make a decision she wouldn't regret, Techniques no. 1 (two or three times a day) and no. 9 (every evening) were counselled, and she was asked to practise them for about a week.

Ten or so days later, she told me:

'The self-hypnosis has worked. I've managed to stand back and look at the alternatives objectively. And I've come to the conclusion I should go back to Lille. That will give me the chance to look after my grandmother. She's 92 now, her health is quite good on the whole, but her sight is getting very poor and my parents don't spend much time with her . . .

'But my decision is, perhaps, only a temporary solution. It doesn't rule out coming back to Paris for good, in a few years' time, when the economic recovery is a reality. Getting back into the tourist industry would be far less problematic then.'

Aggression

Anita I., aged 37, admitted:

'My boss is right, some days I do get aggressive with the customers. It's not easy to keep your temper when you work at the box office in a cinema which, especially towards the end of the week, has a certain kind of clientèle. All the young people come up from the suburbs in gangs and cause a disturbance even before they get inside! . . .'

By using Technique no. 27, this patient learned self-control and avoided the dismissal her boss was threatening.

Laziness

Roger R., aged 27, said:

'I haven't really stirred myself for a long time. My colleagues who started at the same time as I did are all managers now, but as far as I'm concerned, I went into administration to get a bit of peace, I haven't ever had any great ambition. My wife doesn't understand me, she just makes fun of me when I tell her I'm taking a philosophical stance, that it's the path to wisdom, she accuses me of being lazy; she wants me to be sitting exams and climbing a career ladder . . .'

So that this patient could become a bit more dynamic, he was invited to try Technique no. 29. And in the interval before he could reap its benefits, Technique no. 9 was practised on a daily basis as a toning-up exercise. Two months after the consultation, Roger R. decided to yield to his wife's wishes!

Inattentiveness

Mireille J., aged 25, confided her problem:

'Just lately, I've been making a number of mistakes at the office. The work isn't complicated, though. I just need to feel less distracted . . . and think less about the problems I'm having with my boyfriend . . .'

Through using Technique no. 26, the patient was able to stop thinking about other things and at the same time her powers of concentration were strengthened by practising Technique no. 7.

As a result her performance at work become irreproachable.

Constant lateness

Jacques B., aged 30, claimed:

'I do hurry . . . it's not my fault if I'm always late . . . With my old boss, I always got by, but this new one doesn't care a damn if I'm the best salesman in the shop, he keeps on and on at me and even sent me a registered letter last week . . .'

When we got down to details, it became obvious that the patient, more or less unconsciously, was trying to put off the moment he had to go in to work for as long as possible, because his present job didn't exactly conform to the type of work he really wanted.

Technique no. 29 helped Jacques B. adopt a more constructive outlook (it eliminated the sense of frustration he felt with the nature of his current work). His resolve 'to do everything to be on time' was reinforced through using Technique no. 26. As a result, from the first week after the consultation, he was late less and less frequently, and then, by the end of about a month, his practice of Technique no. 29 was having results: he ended up being one of those who regularly got to work really early.

Lack of patience

Julie S., aged 44, complained:

'My life's become hell! Everything started going wrong when they introduced a new system into the scientific research laboratory where I work. I've never learned anything about computers, and now I have to work on computer-aided design. Our electronic engineers are planning printed circuits to detect particles after nuclear testings. My job is to produce the printed circuit and the set-up for the components and the sorting, following a plan worked out by them. It's complex, difficult work which requires an enormous amount of patience and absolute concentration.

'What's really getting on my nerves, and I find this quite exasperating, is the fact that my so-calling team-mate refuses to let me tap into his expertise to help me out. He's very up to date in his knowledge of this process, but he just leaves me to get out of my own mess, and takes no notice if I ask him to explain something. Friends have advised me to go and talk to the director. But I daren't. It could be used against me. I would rather they didn't think I was incompetent . . .

'The truth is that nothing will ever make me like this kind of work. I wanted to do something artistic, but I married very young, right after secondary school. For about twelve years I was a captive wife, bringing up a family, and that was it. We were equally to blame for our divorce, but it put me in a terribly difficult situation. I was given custody of our two children, and so I had to get a job. Luckily I had relatives who helped me land this job in the laboratory. Now I'm neither the right age, nor do I have the qualifications to find a job elsewhere. I'll have to stick it out where I am until I reach retirement age.

'Neither my son nor my daughter earns enough yet to be able to go off and find even a bedsit. They are still living with me. When I get home after work I feel exhausted and irritable, and I simply haven't the patience to put up with their temperamental behaviour and odd habits. We're always having rows. Our life together is made even worse by the fact that we only have two main rooms in our small flat. We're always on top of each other, someone wants to do this, someone else wants to do that, we can never agree, whether it's a programme on television or something else. I can never have any peace. And so I sleep badly and then it's even more difficult to find the patience to do my work properly.'

Julie S. was advised to practise Technique no. 1 (mental and physical revitalisation, to restore peace of mind), Technique no. 5 (increasing powers of concentration) and, most importantly, Technique no. 17 (to combat impatience). One or more of these exercises had to be done every day, depending on what opportunity she had, and in the first week they had to be done at least twice a day.

The following month, Julie S. gave me her news:

'I feel as though I've been on holiday. I still find my work extremely tiresome, but I manage to concentrate on it without too much effort. It's all going better at home too. I find it easier coping with all the strains of the three of us living together. My sleep has improved, I begin the day in a good mood, something that hasn't happened to me for goodness knows how long . . .'

A sense of discouragement

Yves L., aged 47, put his case to me:

'I'm paying dearly for something stupid I did. You see, I'm a craftsman. I make fancy jewellery, and I had an exclusive contract with a wholesaler, who sold it on to outlets here and abroad. Last January he took on a pleasant sort of woman called Claire as a replacement for the buyer, who was retiring.

'At first, everything went well, just as it had in the past. Every month, I had my small order. By the way, I should tell you that I've never gone out of my way to get rich. What's important to me is my freedom, even if it means not earning very much. Anyway, as I was saying, everything was going well, I had no cause to mourn the departure of the other female buyer who had always made the selection from my designs before.

'Then, one fine day – or perhaps I should say, one

179

ill-fated day – I asked Claire if she would like to go to the theatre, I thought it would put our business relations on a firmer footing. She accepted, very happily. The following evening I met her at the theatre, where they were putting on a very funny play. In the interval I asked Claire if she'd like a drink and we went to the bar. She was radiant and in a really good mood. Then, I noticed an extremely pretty woman, who was also having a drink at the bar. Our eyes met and she gave me a smile. Being an inveterate woman-chaser, I asked Claire to excuse me and quickly went over to introduce myself to the woman. We talked for a few minutes and I had no problem extracting her telephone number . . . Once I'd done that, I went back to Claire, and told her the woman was an old acquaintance but we'd lost touch. She didn't believe me. Her attitude changed. I could sense she was angry with me. Then the penny dropped: she must have imagined, quite wrongly, that I had an ulterior motive in asking her out . . .

'After the play finished, I took her home in the car. All very gentlemanly. Throughout the journey, she never said a word. When we got to her flat, she thanked me for the lovely evening and we went our separate ways.

'Three weeks later, at the time I normally delivered my order, I waited for Claire to give me her new order for the following month, as usual. But she told me: "What you've brought will be enough for the moment, come and see us again a month from now, and things will perhaps be clearer." So I waited a month, and then went to see her in her office, and took a beautiful bunch of flowers. A waste of money. No order that month either. She told me: "I think you'll have to change your collection entirely." Why not? I prepared new designs and went and showed them to her. She grimaced: "They're corny, not at all what we're looking for . . ."

'So twice she'd reacted the same way. It was as plain as a pike staff – she was getting her revenge. I decided to take my grievances to the boss. "I'm sorry," he said, "but Madame Claire has my entire backing for what she chooses or doesn't choose to buy. If she thinks that your designs aren't suitable for us any more, then I'll have to go along with her." Then I told him what had happened. He laughed: "Poor thing, she doesn't have a clue she's not your type. If you'd slept with her, you wouldn't be in this mess now . . .

' "Why don't you try to get back into her good books by asking her out again?" No, I knew I couldn't possibly make love to her, even if, and it wasn't very likely, she gave me the opportunity. There was absolutely nothing about her that turned me on.

'Now the truth has dawned. My enemy not only no longer wants any more of my work, but she's getting regular supplies from one of my competitors. I have lost my most important customer for good. And it's no joke. I could of course always go straight to the retailers. But working through a rep's against my principles. If I want it done properly I'll have to visit the shops myself with my samples. The problem is that I have neither the courage nor the patience. The bitchy trick she played on me has totally unnerved me . . .'

So that Yves L. could put his bad luck behind him and do the necessary calls to get his jewellery into the shops, he was advised to practise Techniques no. 13 and no. 1 for a week. Then, to give him the patience he would need in making contact with his (eventual) new customers, he was also recommended to use Technique no. 17, three times a day for the first ten days and once in the mornings thereafter for as long as he needed to.

The result: The patient's dynamism returned and he got used to spending his time both making his fancy jewellery and selling it.

Sport

The transformation that self-hypnosis can produce for those involved in sport is particularly striking as the following case histories testify:

Bad temper

Louis D., aged 62, had this to say:

'I'd been diagnosed as having arthritis in my spine and my sciatic nerve often gave me atrocious pain. Once, for two whole months, I simply couldn't move. The rheumatologist told me afterwards that I would have to get used to the idea of walking with a stick. The thought revolted me. I slammed out of his surgery and went to an osteopath. It was the best thing I could have done. As you can see for yourself, I manage to walk quite normally. I have two or three sessions with the osteopath once a year, as a preventive measure, and everything's fine. I also go swimming, which explains why I look as good as I do.

'Yes, well, I'd never done any sport in my life before, and now I go swimming – backstroke – every day, for a good half-hour. It was my osteopath who advised me to do it. I can never thank him enough.

'I usually go swimming between midday and three, in a

very pleasant pool near my home. But for the last three weeks, with some reluctance. Because there's a bloke of about thirty, hefty, a real sporty type, who always gets up my wick – if you'll excuse the expression. He charges blindly along and always knocks into me. And he never even bothers to say sorry. Other swimmers, and I'm no exception, will always say it quite automatically if they bump into someone.

'I change direction when I see him coming. But wherever I happen to be in the pool, he always finds a way, sooner or later, of banging into my arms or my legs. Being on the short-tempered side anyway, obviously I'm tempted to punch him in the face . . . Only common sense has stopped me so far. He's the sort who'd laugh in my face, treat me like an old fool. He might even wait for me at the exit for a punch-up. Or he might spy on me, see which my car is, and one day, I'd find all my tyres flat.

'So what should I do? Change swimming pool? The one I go to is the only one in my area, the others are too far away. And who knows? If I did go somewhere else, I might bump into another rowdy character like him there too.

'Up to now, by making a superhuman effort, I've managed to control my temper, I content myself with gnashing my teeth every time he bumps into me. Only it's becoming more and more difficult. The time will come when I won't be able to restrain myself and there'll be ructions. Perhaps your famous self-hypnosis can help me . . .'

Techniques no. 10 and 12 were advised (each to be practised two or three times daily), and after only ten days or so Louis D. told me:

'It's not a problem any more. Your exercises have been like a magic potion. Can you imagine, thanks to them, I was able to make my peace with that chap I was telling you about. Last Thursday I spoke to him. Without a hint of hostility . . . Hypocritically I asked him to tell me the secret of his magnificent physique, what other sports besides swimming could have developed such muscles. To my great surprise, he answered me very politely and told me about his judo, volleyball and mountaineering. Then I told him I would be really grateful if he didn't swim quite so violently. He promised he would try. Now he does take care. And, most surprisingly of all, we greet each other in friendly fashion and exchange a few words every day . . . except Monday, when the pool's closed.'

Down in the dumps

Fabien J., aged 21, told me:

'I've been mad about tennis since I was a child. For five years in a row, from 1982 to 1987, I was in championship competitions, first regional ones, then the national championships. Always on the up and up . . . Until six months ago I was beaten. It was a shock for me . . . You know, when I read that passage in Caesar's *Gallic Wars*, where he says to one of his comrades in arms that he'd rather be the most important man in a small village in Helvetia than have a second-rate post in Rome, it was easy for me to understand, because I've always thought the same . . . And now I don't have the courage to go on . . .'

One session of hypnosis laid the foundations for a 'relaunch'. Then, using Technique no. 27, Fabien learned to overcome his vanity and go back to playing, despite the promise he'd made to himself never to play again. And it didn't take long for a win to make him completely forget the effect that being beaten had had on him.

Bon viveur

Paul D., aged 25, was well aware of his problem:

'I just can't manage to go without all the good things before a match. I know it stops me giving my best performance, but I don't care, I think it's stupid giving up a good meal and sex . . . Only, if I go on like this, the team might be demoted because of me . . .'

By practising Technique no. 29, Paul was able to exert the self-discipline he needed and pursue his career as a professional footballer.

Lack of resolve

Veronique P., aged 24, told me:
    'In theory, there's nothing I'd like more than to do all the training that I've been told I should do. But, often at the last minute, it becomes a moot point. And instead of slogging my guts out, I'm inclined not to complicate my life . . .'

Technique no. 26 offered Veronique P. a means of ridding herself of the habit of always choosing the easy option: she has resolved to find a way round the difficulties and overcome them, and nowadays she always manages to attend the training sessions on which her participation in the swimming championships depend.

Emotional Life

Self-hypnosis can help you considerably in facing up to the responsibilities that go hand in hand with being a father, mother, husband, wife, lover and so on. It will enable you to carry out your obligations under optimum conditions, as you will see from the following few case histories . . .

Reticence

Charles A., aged 44, explained:

'When I get home, I'm all in, it's too much effort to talk. Both my children and my wife reproach me for not saying a word at dinner and being just as taciturn on my days off. My feeling is that there's no sense in making them share my worries, but they don't seem to understand, they think I don't love them any more . . .'

After practising Technique no. 26, Charles A. was able to overcome his reticence and open up to his family. The result was a very definite improvement in their relations.

Jealousy

Gisèle E., aged 42, told me:

'My husband hasn't been himself for about a year now. I get the feeling that he's less and less interested in me and goes through the physical motions just to reassure me, while all the time he's thinking about another woman. He says I'm mad, I've no reason to be jealous, but if I continue to "poison his existence" with my accusations, he really will be unfaithful . . .'

By using Technique no. 28, Gisèle E. learned to control her feelings and no longer inflict jealous outbursts upon her husband.

As a result the couple were able to return to the harmonious understanding they had previously enjoyed.

Possessiveness

Yvette C., aged 39, complained:

'My son, who's 16, has started to hate me. He sleeps away from home more and more often and is threatening to go and live with a girl who's got her clutches into him. And all this just because I dared to tell him she wasn't suitable for him! It's not the first time it's happened either. Last year, he almost left for ever because of some other tart.'

With Technique no. 26, this possessive mother was helped to become an 'enlightened mother', and once she ceased her constant criticism of his son's dates, all friction between them disappeared.

Insensitivity

François M., aged 47, confided:

'Both my marriages wound up in divorce. I've lived alone for the last six years. And the few relationships and numerous affairs I'd had since have given me no cause to regret it. I swore I'd never fall into that trap again. Living with someone or, even worse, marrying them, isn't for me, thank you very much!

'The AIDS scare has obliged me to give up sleeping around for good. That's why if I fall for a woman I like, I'm not in so much hurry to get rid of her. But that doesn't mean . . . I still do my best not to get attached to her. In other words, I only want a purely physical relationship, without all the sentimental hoo-ha.

'I met Anna at some friends'. She's Polish, a doctor – so that was reassuring for a start: I didn't need to worry about AIDS with her, at least, not too much. After we'd been out a few times, we got down to the main business. She was very passionate, but refined at the same time, and she satisfied me right from our first sexual contact. We've been seeing each other now for about eight months – two or three times a week. We've even gone off on short trips together. I'm the one who doesn't want us to spend more than four or five days together at a time. Once, I told her straight – I couldn't have made it clearer – that I absolutely had to keep my freedom. It didn't seem to bother her.

'But you can't really trust women. Just recently, I've had a feeling that Anna seems to be trying very hard to make me change my mind. She's swamping me with affection that I don't think I need. It's as though, with all her sensual pleasuring, she's trying to make me love her not just physically. I've resisted her tactics well and truly, and now she's reproaching me for being insensitive. She wants me to be interested in her problems at work and other things, and share her interests, like classical music, the mountains, Slavonic literature. I can do without all that.

'Quite honestly, the extraordinary sexual understanding I've discovered with Anna has robbed me of my normal reactions. In similar circumstances I wouldn't hesitate to break it off with another woman. But with her, I somehow can't do it. I'd like to keep on with her – not that I'd want it to degenerate into an "indestructible bond". But unfortunately I'm not succeeding in giving her what she would like me to give her. When she wants me to read Tolstoy, or go to a concert with her, or to the Alps for a fortnight, or, even worse, have a "quiet evening" in, and spend more time exchanging ideas rather than playing bedtime games, I feel myself withdrawing. I leave her with the feeling that I never want to see her again. But the next day or the day after that, I can't keep it up. Just picking up the telephone and hearing her voice is enough to give me an erection . . .'

Using Technique no. 27, François M. managed to achieve sufficient patience to be able to accommodate his partner's 'whims'. So their relationship has withstood the test of time . . . without the two of them being in any (apparent) danger of ending up living together!

Sex

Hypnotherapy in medical practice has had exceptional success in dealing with impotence and frigidity. Self-hypnosis is a reliable aid for men and women in a variety of problems that can harm the quality of the sexual act or simply sexual understanding ...

Absence

Alice W., aged 35, confided:

'My partner is more and more unhappy because, as he says, "I'm just not there when we make love" ... Actually, he's not far off the mark. I have quite a lot of worries connected with work at the moment. So I don't show as much enthusiasm as I used to in the past. It's also difficult for me to have an orgasm ...'

By using Techniques nos. 1 and 27 in tandem, Alice W. was able to relax, something she needed very much to do, and so was able to stop thinking about her problems while they were making love.

Shyness

Laurent R., aged 23, told me:

'Beautiful women have always intimidated me. I don't know how it happens, but if a girl is pretty, it inhibits me, or almost, but there's no problem at all with fairly plain girls . . .'

Laurent was advised to learn Technique no. 29 and, meanwhile, while he was familiarising himself properly with this method, he practised Technique no. 2 several times a day. After less than two weeks, he had no more problems.

Being absurd

Renée T., aged 37, thought:

'All porn films should be banned on television. Ever since my husband saw them, he wants us to do the same . . . Frankly, it doesn't do anything for me. But he goes on insisting and insisting, he claims I'm being absurd and puritanical, and that I'm old-fashioned and riddled with prejudice, and I've had enough. We're quarrelling all the time. What I'm really afraid of is that he'll start looking somewhere else for what he's not getting from me. If only you could help me be less obstinate . . .'

Renée T. managed to overcome her reticence by using Technique no. 28.

Sadism

Nicolas H., aged 45, remembered:

'I had nothing to complain about with my ex-wife on that particular issue. She was quite masochistic, and didn't seem to mind me being the way I was from time to time. But apart from that, there wasn't much understanding between us, and we ended up getting a divorce. I remarried a year and a half ago. My new wife is full of good qualities, she's a dream wife. I wouldn't do anything in the world to lose her. That's why I've never mentioned what I call my "whims" to her. I'd certainly never dare go on to do it. For good reason. Perhaps I'm wrong, but I think she'd be so shocked, she'd find it difficult to understand . . . The problem is that now when I feel excited, really excited, it's becoming more and more difficult to hold back. I'm always afraid I won't be able to stop myself hitting her, brutalising her. You know, it's not really anything to do with wanting to hurt her or getting pleasure from making her suffer. The excitement is in the gestures themselves and hearing the screams they produce. That sort of thing really turns me on, it makes me so full of joy. And so to come to the point, is there any way I can continue to keep my urges under control? . . .'

By using Technique no. 29, Nicolas H. was able to keep his promise to himself and not put his marriage in jeopardy by revealing his tendencies.

Irritation

Didier P., aged 42, confided:

'I never married. It was because of my parents: they detested each other and ruined my childhood and my adolescence. It's amazing I didn't grow up gay . . .

'Because I work in show business – I'm an impresario – I have lots of opportunities. I'm not exaggerating when I say I could have as many women as I want. But for the last ten years or so, I've preferred quality to quantity. In my youth I'd change partners as often as I changed my shirt, but now I have quite long-lasting relationships. For example, my affair with my last mistress went on for nearly three years. Her doctor had warned her not to take the Pill. That meant I had to use a condom. It didn't bother me, because she used to unroll them over my penis very delicately, and fondle me all the time she was doing it. And we'd reach this stage only after quite a while; we'd put it on just when I was ready to come.

'For a number of reasons our relationship finished seven or eight months ago. Ever since, I've been incapable of having a normal sex life. You'll see why. At my age, after a very full sex life, it's impossible to get used to having to put on a condom. Obviously, I can't ask women who would really like to sleep with me, to show me a doctor's certificate or the results of a lab test to prove they haven't got AIDS. And there's no question of me taking risks. All I can do is put on a condom right at the start. My problem stems from that.

'A few days after I broke off with Monique, my last mistress, the one I was talking about, I went out with a really nice young singer. The evening ended, as it should, at my place. Without going into it in detail, she let me kiss her, then undress her. I asked her to put my condom on for me. She didn't want to. She said it was my job. A matter of a few seconds, you might say. I won't argue with you. But it only took those few seconds for me to lose my erection! . . .

'We spent the night together, kissing and fondling. I got another hard-on. But when the moment came to put on the condom again, I was back where I started. In the end she took pity on me and decided to do what Monique did. Nothing changed. Finally we got to sleep. When I woke up in the morning I had an erection. I hurriedly put on the condom. The same. The moment my penis came into contact with it, it went limp.

'Well this first setback didn't put me off, as you might imagine. There were other women, young and not so young, all beautiful and desirable. But it was the same every time, I'd get rattled and lose the "wherewithal". Every time. Without exception. In fact, I only have to think about using a condom and I feel queasy and full of apprehension. At the crucial moment I get too irritated, I know it's totally impossible to put on this condom properly. I tried again and again, but the very moment I began to put it on, my penis went from hard to soft . . . It's sad to say it, but I don't think I'll dare try again.'

The patient was advised to use Techniques nos. 15 and 17, two or three times a day over a week (so that they would be properly learned), then do them again just before he knew he was going to have sex. The blockage disappeared, as Didier told me:

'I'm back in the land of the living! While I was putting on the condom, the erection went down a bit, it's true, but I managed to get inside, and after that, all my old vitality returned . . .'

Victim of routine

Jocelyne O., aged 38, revealed:
'I'm very worried, because if things continue as they are, it'll destroy my happiness. You see, when I married the first time I was 22. Jean, my husband, adored me and at first everything was marvellous. Then he got more and more demanding. I'd rather not talk about the details. They were fantasies and I was really shocked. Then he started claiming I wasn't interested in sex. Perhaps he was right. In any case, he went off and found someone else to give him what I didn't want to, or more accurately what I couldn't give him. And we got a divorce.

'I've known François, my second husband, for six years. But we only married four years ago. He doesn't have such outlandish ideas about sex. We have similar tastes and we get on very well on an emotional level. Our relationship has been strengthened by the birth of our daughter, Lucie, who's now two . . . it's a relationship that's been perfect ever since we first met.

'I presume that it's the same for a lot of other women too, but, after a certain number of years, when you're together, in a situation similar to ours, and it's nothing to do with the love I feel for my husband, I feel less and less inclined to have physical relations with him. There was a time when, if he touched me, it had an almost immediate effect. I could give myself to him entirely and sincerely. Now it's rarely like that. When he takes me in his arms and starts wanting to arouse me, I already know what he's going to start saying, what he's going to do, minute by minute. It's giving me a mental block. I don't feel any desire at all. Especially after a day at work when things haven't gone very well, or I'm worried about my daughter or my mother's health or whatever.

'Now, François doesn't notice anything, but I've had to start pretending, and I hate doing that. I groan with pleasure and say things to make him believe I'm enjoying it too. I'm ashamed about it. What's worst is pretending I'm having an orgasm. I really hate myself when I do that.

'If only my husband could decide on some changes! Change the words he uses, and not always do everything in exactly the same order. Perhaps just a few modifications would make it easier for me to go along with him.

'Who knows how it will end? I fear the worst. Either he'll cotton on that I'm faking it, or I'll become incapable of hiding the truth. Often I'm on the point of telling him I'm not keen any more. But I shut up. I don't want to hurt him. And I also keep my secret because I'm afraid. François loves me with all his heart, I'm sure of it. But, if he finds out about my non-receptiveness, he might do what my first husband did and start looking at other women.'

Jocelyne O. agreed to practise Technique no. 16 on a daily basis, and was able to revitalise her sexuality. Thanks to the use of Technique no. 14 in tandem, she managed to conquer her innate shyness and dared to ask her husband to take a few 'anti-routine' measures . . .

Everyday Life

To end these case histories, here are a few that show how self-hypnosis and similar techniques can be useful in a variety of situations . . .

Road rage

Thierry P., aged 42, said:

'I could never have imagined that I would become aggressive. Until three years ago I lived in the country and everything was fine. It took being transferred to Paris for me to change, little by little . . . You see, what with going to the office and my business appointments, I spend three or four hours a day behind the wheel. The morning's fairly OK, then the tension starts building up and up. If there's the slightest hint that another motorist is trying to get the better of me, or if a car's going too slow in front, I get into such a rage, I rant and rave and sometimes I even feel I might go further than that . . . Until now I've succeeded in avoiding a set-to. But who knows how long it's going to last? It could well be that one day or other I'm going to see red and something truly awful will happen. So, what can you advise, so that I don't end up under lock and key or in hospital?'

196

To start with, Technique no. 2, and then, after he had learned it properly, Technique no. 29 allowed Thierry P. moments of relaxation which helped diminish his aggression. Lately, after practising Technique no. 29 twice a day, he has succeeded in reaching a state of total calm:

'I'm now immune to even the dirtiest tricks drivers get up to,' he says.

Spendthrift

Nathalie C., aged 37, complained:

'I've quite a tight budget, and yet I can't be sensible. I buy lots of things which, in reality, I don't honestly need. And my husband's in despair with me, obviously . . .'

Once she became adept at self-hypnosis, by practising Technique no. 6 every day, Nathalie C. succeeded in putting up an insuperable barrier between herself and the media, which could take the blame for encouraging her reckless spending.

Hostility

Noemi S., aged 34, explained:

'I work in public relations. That means I have to be all sweetness and smiles, and patient, all day long. At present this is pretty difficult because my daughter is giving me a lot of bother, and my husband's on the point of leaving me. Once I finish work, I'm too exhausted to keep the mask on, and the hostility I feel towards the whole human race comes to the surface. I don't make any effort to be nice when I'm in the Métro, or doing my shopping, or even when I'm at home, I just spitefully work off my frustrations. At this rate I may well end up being just as unpleasant to my colleagues and clients . . .'

Techniques nos. 1 and 3 helped give this patient momentary relaxation while she waited for Technique no. 29 to have an effect, and in fact at the end of three weeks' practice, she had built up an indestructible barrier against her aggressive tendencies.

A fiery temper

Richard L., aged 55, reckoned:

'By the time you're in your fifties, it's impossible to lose the habits of a lifetime. As far as I'm concerned, whenever something gets on my nerves, I've always ranted and raged and that releases the tension, and then it's over and done with. I don't think about it any more. If my car won't start, I let fly a few expletives, loud and clear. And that's it. I calm down then. If by chance someone bumps into me in a public place, I don't care if they take me for a madman, I really sound off at them, then my bile evaporates and I can smile and so avoid any unpleasant repercussions.

'My parents, friends, colleagues and everyone who knows me well don't bother about it. They know what I'm like, that I've a quick temper. And as for others, I've always managed in the past to get out of it still in their good books. Of course, there are people who get annoyed with me for being like that, but my method of unwinding has never brought me any real problems.

'But now, things have changed. From one day to the next I risk getting myself arrested for murder . . . No, I'm not exaggerating. My wife will confirm it, it's becoming harder and harder to control myself, and not strangle the load of garbage who's poisoning my life. He's a retired civil servant. As ugly and shifty as they come. He's been living in our block of flats for the last six or seven months. But he's already given me such a hard time, I feel as though I've had him on my back since the dawn of creation.

'It began with the birds. None of my neighbours have ever grumbled. But he went and complained to the landlord, then the public hygiene department at the Council. I was in trouble because I was feeding the sparrows and pigeons on my balcony. I suppose he would rather they died of hunger.

'We have a garage for the tenants. Sometimes I wash my car there, or rather I wipe it down with a damp cloth. There again, it's never bothered any of my neighbours. This pig, though, has informed the landlord and I'll shortly be receiving a registered letter . . .

'At one time, we were always having burglaries. In the flats, the basement and the garage, they took hubcaps, spare wheels, things left on the car seats or in the boot. I got a German Shepherd dog from the Animal Protection Society. The other dogs in the flats are little things: he's the only one you could say has got any bottle. In fact, since I've had him, we've had far fewer visits from burglars. That hasn't stopped that son of a bitch from being the one behind the registered letters I'm getting from the landlord, telling me that my dog's barking is disturbing everybody in the building and that it's got to stop.

'The other thing is I'm a night owl. I never go to bed early. Which means I take my bath after midnight. My new neighbour couldn't wait to inform me that the noise from the pipes wakes him up. Just for once he wrote it in a letter addressed direct to me . . . It put me in a rage right off. But thinking that perhaps it was civil of him not to complain to the landlord, I decided to be nice to him and took a quick, simple shower instead of my bath. This concession wasn't enough for him. Shortly afterwards, even though there are two floors between us, he claimed that the noise from my television was preventing him from sleeping. This time, instead of raising the issue direct with me, he went to the landlord again. I felt I wanted to stamp on him, like a cockroach . . .

'It's the last straw that breaks the camel's back. The other day we met in the lift. He greeted me in his sanctimonious way as if butter wouldn't melt in his mouth, then made an offensive remark because the smoke from my cigarette was annoying him. That was it. I couldn't take any more. I shouted at him. I told him his lack of tolerance was beginning to try my patience sorely. He made the mistake of shouting back. If he hadn't done that, things might have stayed as they were. But his attitude and his insults – just when I was about to lower my tone – made me see red and I punched him. He left with his nose bleeding and saying I'd be hearing from him shortly.

'The day after, down at the police station where I was charged with "assault and grievous bodily harm", I didn't deny it. In the state I'm in a fine doesn't bother me . . . What worries me is the prospect of our next encounter. Inevitably, one of these days, we're going to run smack into each other, in the lift or the garage, or the main hall. And I doubt whether I'll be able to ignore him, I might well end up smashing his head in or strangling him . . .'

By using Technique no. 10 intensively, Richard L. managed to avoid a charge of murder, or even attempted murder.

Grief

Jacques S., aged 44, confided:

'My mother died on 3 February last. I was her only son. You can imagine how, loving me so much, it was a difficult death. And it was difficult for me too. She was the best friend I ever had, I confided everything in her, she was like a little sister to me – she always acted and thought like a young girl, always happy and optimistic, always looking on the world wide-eyed . . .

'My father passed away with duodenal cancer eight years ago. He adored me too, he always spoilt me, never denied me anything to make me happy. His death shook me, really shook me. I believe that if my mother hadn't still been alive at the time, I might have committed suicide, because I was already under great strain with problems at work and other worries too.

'I have to say that both my father and my mother had begun to complain of symptoms years and years before when it would not have been too late to treat them properly. But the doctors attending them – their GPs – didn't bother to investigate them. They just gave prescription after prescription, without really looking into a deeper cause for their intermittent tiredness, their digestive problems and other anomalies. In the end, my father had had enough and went to a specialist. That's how, after a simple scan, the exact nature of his illness was diagnosed. But by then it was impossible to find appropriate treatment. With my mother it was the same. When she was so exasperated by the doctor attending her, I went to a consultant in gastroenterology, and he told me that the cancer in her liver was too far advanced to be able to do anything.

'As I said, after my father died, I didn't put an end to my life, simply because I still had my mother. Now that she's gone too, the only thing holding me back is my girlfriend, whom I'm fairly attached to, except that she's married, and some days I can't help wondering if my disappearance would make much difference to her, she wouldn't take long to find another lover to console her, what's to stop her?

'The fact is, I no longer feel any joy in living. The day after my mother died I asked my employer for unlimited leave. It's been almost seven months since I've worked now. The days go by without my doing anything constructive. I don't budge from the house. I just lie or sit, incapable of making up my mind even about whether to read a book or watch television. I just think about my parents all the time. I still get a feeling of revulsion when I think about the doctors who didn't even take the trouble to find out what was wrong with them in time. And I blame myself. Yes, I reproach myself for not having taken the initiative. I should have insisted on having them examined by specialists at a time when it would have been possible to save them, or at least prolong their lives a little, and then I would have spared them all that useless suffering in the last months of their lives.'

In order for this patient to be able to overcome his lethargy, he was advised to follow the revitalising Technique no. 19, and then to try Technique no. 18 – the one that includes 'automatic writing'.

The day after our appointment, Jacques S. told me:

'My mother responded to my call! She hasn't totally abandoned me. I have proof. You know, she was brought up in England, and English was always the language she preferred. And, if you can believe it, I could make out the words "Cheer up"! And that's not all. When I compared the automatic writing with one of her letters, the writing was the same!'

A Few Final Words

One could of course cite many other case histories to show you how useful self-hypnosis is, but we have run out of space, and to come full circle, let us return to its parent, 'hypnosis', whose history the world over has been characterised by periods when it has been very fashionable and periods when it has been discredited.

The principal detractors of hypnosis were the neurologist Babinski, who based his criticisms on work done by Charcot at the Salpêtrière Hospital (justly criticised), as well as Freud and his disciples, who were following, as we know now, a completely different, much longer path.

But, even while, in Austria, Freud, 'forgetting' that psychoanalysis derived from hypnosis, was particularly hostile towards it, in France Pierre Janet[1] was drawing the attention of medical circles to its benefits: he was a pioneer of revelatory hypnosis – that is to say, of hypnosis intended to establish the deep causes of psychosomatic illness. Through hypnosis he succeeded in discovering the cause of blindness in one of his patients, who showed no signs of

---

[1] Pierre Janet was the first psychologist to make the connection between academic psychology and the clinical treatment of mental illness. He specialised in hysteria, obsession, amnesia and personality.

having any organic lesions, and through this demonstration, as well as other similar ones, he was able to show that by destroying traumatic memories buried in the unconscious, a cure could be effected.

The importance of suggestion

Paradoxically, Freud paid homage to hypnosis by translating Bernheim's work on suggestion into German.

Now Bernheim and Liebault, who founded the School of Nancy, were to prove that it is suggestion that is the key to hypnosis, and not the passes dear to magnetisers or the visual fixation that the early hypnotists believed to be essential to procuring a hypnotic state.

And in fact, because suggestion is the really crucial factor on which hypnosis depends, we can better understand why it is so useful in self-hypnosis, which operates entirely by suggestion.

So, the development that led from magnetism to hypnotism, then to suggestion as the key factor in modern hypnosis, ended up with autosuggestion, then, finally, self-hypnosis, thus dethroning the 'hypnotist-king' of conventional hypnosis. The people who have had an important role in this progression are Oskar Vogt, Schultz and Coue.

A wish

Two people among the most celebrated scientists of our age have spoken highly of the merits of hypnosis: the Russian Pavlov (Nobel prizewinner in 1904) and the Frenchman Charles Richet (Nobel prizewinner in 1913). The Columbian Professor Caycedo also took his inspiration from it when in the late Sixties he founded the latest fashionable therapy, 'Sophrology'.

It would be good if, with such precedents as these, further scientific research could be set in motion into hypnosis and self-hypnosis: since they are verifiable, these two methods in fact meet all the criteria demanded of a science, and a better knowledge of their virtues would be nothing less than helpful to mankind.